W9-AEC-424

THE ESSENCE OF BUDDHISM

39

JOHN WALTERS

The Essence of Buddhism

THOMAS Y. CROWELL COMPANY

New York, Established 1834

Originally published in Great Britain
under the title *Mind Unshaken.*

Designed by Laurel Wagner
Manufactured in the United States of America.
Library of Congress Catalog Card No. 62-12809

Apollo Edition 1964

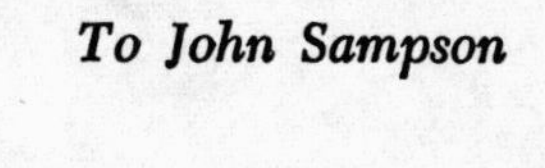

To John Sampson

CONTENTS

THE ESSENCE OF BUDDHISM

INTRODUCTION

This is a book for ordinary practical people and not for highly sensitive mystics. It offers the religion or philosophy of Buddhism in the clearest possible form, without masses of baffling words in Pali or Sanskrit, without phrases so purple that they are incomprehensible. Buddhism is, after all, no religion of mystery. Countless millions of simple folk over thousands of years have been guided from the cradle to the grave by its kindly light. Then, today, the pure Buddhism of the Theravada school is still the religion of millions of happy people who live in Ceylon, Burma, Thailand, and Cambodia.

In this book I am telling the story of the Buddha and explaining his philosophy while making every effort to exclude anything that might be mere fable or superstition. To succeed in this objective is not always possible, for Buddhism is so ancient a religion that the legendary must often have become inextricably tangled with the real. Scholars have faced the same difficulties in their endeavors to separate the authentic stories of Jesus and Mohammed from the inventions of excited or superstitious imaginations. But I am, above all, endeavoring to show how Buddhist principles might solve our own problems and enlighten our lives in these perplexing modern times.

I want to stress that my book concentrates upon the Buddhism of the Theravada or Hinayana school. It neither endorses nor condemns the complex and elaborate Mahayana systems of Japan, China, and Korea or the Tantrism of Tibet. Definitely it offers no comfort, consolation, or encouragement to "beatniks" and other eccentrics who have distorted the Zen system of Buddhist philosophy into a gospel of self-indulgence and depravity.

This *Essence of Buddhism* is not the work of a mystic or professional scholar but of a former newspaperman who, surveying an adventurous career, regards Buddhism as the greatest "story" he ever encountered. I had from youth been an amateur student of comparative religion. And on my world travels I had studied Buddhism with a cold indifference, in the belief that Christianity was the only religion that had anything useful to offer to mankind. Then, one day, while I was on a visit to Bangkok in Thailand, the message of Buddhism suddenly enlightened my mind. This enlightenment came after long reflection and after long talks with Buddhist friends, and it was followed by a period of study and inquiry among Buddhists in Ceylon. Today I find it hard to believe that once I sneered at Buddhism as a defeatist philosophy of pessimism and hopelessness, a primitive form of Existentialism. For these are the Four Noble Truths that form the foundation of the Buddha's teachings:

1. The Noble Truth concerning suffering
2. The Noble Truth concerning the arising of suffering

3. The Noble Truth concerning the cessation of suffering
4. The Noble Truth concerning the way to the cessation of suffering

What do these four Truths—which formerly seemed so depressing to me—mean?

Human life and, indeed, all life is dominated by suffering. This suffering is caused by craving, greed, attachment, or desires which are never satisfied. This suffering can cease only when craving and other appetites of infatuation are stopped or rigidly controlled. And this is made possible by following what the Buddhists call the Noble Eightfold Path of conduct. Then will come peace and eventually a hazily defined state of being or non-being known as Nibbana (or Nirvana). On the other hand, wandering from the Eightfold Path and a continuation of attachments and craving will lead only to rebirth with more of the intolerable sufferings of existence.

In this book the teachings of the Buddha will be explained and discussed at length. But first I shall answer the question that I am so often asked: "What were your thoughts when you moved from orthodox Christianity into Buddhism?" These were hardly constructive thoughts, and doubtless William James would have found them unworthy of even a few lines in his *Varieties of Religious Experience.* I breathed deeply for the first time in the intellectual freedom of pure Buddhism. In its rarefied air I gave the Christianity of the churches a hypercritical look. In my thoughts I sneered at the blunders or crimes of the churches and their leaders in past ages, forgetting that there must have been many simple Christians who were faithful to the true Gospel of Jesus in every age. I contemptuously reviewed and rejected Christian dogma until, eventually, I remembered that one of the greatest glories of Buddhism is its tolerance. For the Buddha compared the man who unjustly condemns other religions to "one who looks up and spits at Heaven. The spittle does not soil Heaven. But it comes back and defiles his own person." However, here is the report of my thoughts as I accepted the message of the Buddha:

The Christian God created heaven and earth and all that therein is. This God is omnipotent. He is also a God of love and compassion and can be approached through prayer. There are pledges in the Gospels that supplications to God will be answered. St. Mark quotes Jesus as promising: "For verily I say unto you, that whosoever shall say unto this mountain, be thou removed, and be thou cast into the sea; and shall not doubt in his heart, but shall believe that those things which he saith shall come to pass; he shall have whatsoever he saith. Therefore I say unto you, what things soever ye desire, when ye pray, believe that ye receive them, and ye shall have them." And men are made in this image of this Loving Father, who sacrificed His only son in order to save them. In the words of one favorite hymn:

Fatherlike He tends and spares us;
Well our feeble frame He knows;
In His arms He gently bears us,
Rescues us from all our foes.

It is all a glorious conception of life and the world. Millions of us profess to believe it. But how many, in their heart of hearts, admit to themselves that it simply isn't true? How many start life believing it, only to be horribly disillusioned and embittered by experience? Who, buffeted by the suffering and sorrow of existence, can seriously claim that God is omnipotent and all-loving? Or that He gives us what we ask for and "rescues us from all our foes"? The origin of the life process is unknown to us because the puny human mind is finite. When told that God created heaven and earth it wonders who created God—and then gets muddled and mixed up. The Buddha, who never pretended to be more than a man, wisely maintained "a noble silence" when asked to answer problems that are beyond human comprehension. He had no slick explanations of the mysteries of eternity or the Ultimate Reality. "The religious life," he said, "does not depend on the dogma that the world is eternal; nor does the religious life depend on the dogma that the world is not eternal. Whether the dogma obtain that the world is eternal or that the world is not eternal, there still remain birth, old age, death, sorrow, lamentation, misery, grief, and despair, for the extinction of which in the present life I am prescribing."

The Buddha taught a doctrine of love and compassion. But never did he make the wild claim that the world was ruled by a supernatural force of love and compassion; for with such an almighty power there could be no evil, no suffering. In the words of Charles Bradlaugh, "The existence of evil is a terrible stumbling block to the Theist. Pain, misery, crime, poverty confront the advocate of eternal goodness and challenge with unanswerable potency his declaration of Deity as all-good, all-wise and all-powerful." And, the great Albert Einstein, said: "If God is omnipotent then every occurrence, including every human action, every human thought and every human feeling and aspiration is also his work; how is it possible to think of holding men responsible for their deeds and thoughts before such an almighty being? In giving our punishments and rewards, he would to a certain extent be passing judgment on himself. How can this be combined with the goodness and righteousness ascribed to him?"

In reality the omnipotent God of Christianity made the lovely red-cheeked child, laughing and playing on the beach. He also made the frail, animalistic idiot child, babbling in the asylum ward. He made the healthy young mother, joyful in husband and family. He also made the young woman screaming with agony in the cancer hospital.

All things bright and beautiful,
The Lord God made them all.

And if He is omnipotent, then He also made all things that are dark and hideous.

Even the most fervent Christians must many times be haunted by the irreverent feeling that God has let them down. For only in theory are his love and mercy all-pervading. In reality these seem quixotic and unstable. Both adults and children are exhorted to put their faith in prayer and in the eternal goodness of God; then their prayers are unanswered and they are visited by evil. Mental turmoil and unbalance results. For their love and trust in the Almighty has, as it were, been betrayed.

In the Korean War I watched the agonies of hundreds of starving, maimed, and wounded children. And, ironically, I heard the children in one improvised war orphanage singing the Korean version of the hymn, "There's a Friend for little children, Above the bright blue sky." And while they sang, U.S. and Chinese planes fought overhead. I was in a Long Island railway wreck where seventy-nine men, women, and children perished on the eve of Thanksgiving Day, dedicated by Americans to gratitude to God for His mercies. Indeed, what has the life of anybody been but an intermittent drama of accident, disease, and death? What is its story but thwarted hope, frustrated ambition, bereavement, weakness, inevitable decline? "Man that is born of woman hath but a short time to live, and is full of misery." The misery is only intensified when he is assured that he is the child of an omnipotent, all-loving God. For this God fails to use His omnipotence to save man from suffering; this God fails to reveal the love with which theologians have credited Him.

All these were my thoughts. And, looking back, I realize that some were uncharitable thoughts and that some of the judgments, made in such circumstances, were perhaps superficial. But to me the paradox was that, in embracing Buddhism, I felt I had come to know the real Jesus Christ. The Buddha, who had no time for theology, superstition, and dogma, caused me to see Jesus without these appendages. I felt that Christianity could become a still better and purer religion if concentration were made upon its teachings of love and forgiveness. And, as time passed, I lost my uncharitableness toward diverse modes of religious expression as I tried increasingly to emulate the tolerance of the Buddha.

As my reflections continued I again pondered on another puzzling feature of the orthodox Christian faith. This was the story that God sent His only begotten Son to die on the Cross in order to atone for the sins of mankind. I had always tried hard to accept this. I had on Good Fridays joined in the long services of sympathy and gratitude to the divine Father and Son for their sacrifice. Sometimes I joined in the ceremony of the Stations of the Cross, meditating sorrowfully but with gratitude for every episode of suffering borne by the Lord on His road to Calvary and finally on the Cross. My sorrow was, I admit, sometimes forced and even insincere. For I would be tempted to think of thousands of ordinary men who had given their lives for ideals, without any fuss being made in their memory. There were our young relatives and friends who in the two World Wars died for "freedom." There were countless Christian martyrs who would have suffered longer and more terrible agonies than did the Christ. Another temptation in my Christian life was to regard the very idea of the sacrificial dogma with repugnance. I saw it as a development of the nauseating and cruel ceremonies in the Jerusalem Temple that Jesus knew so well. At the Passover there were the relays of worshippers with their helpless lambs. The lambs were killed, with rows of priests catching the blood in gold and silver bowls. As each lamb was flayed and offered at the Altar, the choir chanted psalms. And the Christian Church acclaimed Jesus as "the Lamb of God that taketh away the sins of the world," thus perpetuating what I was tempted to regard as a sadistic superstition. Yet, on the other hand, this was a comforting tale to believe. It meant that evil-doing would not have serious consequences so long as the sinner appealed for clemency to the God who had died to save sinners.

There was certainly no such comfort in Buddhism. The Buddha was no god who would grant absolution for the remission of sins. The Buddha could warn; he could not save. Indeed the gulf between Christianity and Buddhism was widest on the problem of sin. In his *Orthodoxy* G. K. Chesterton had written, "All humanity does agree that we are in a net of sin. Most of humanity agrees that there is some way out. But as to what is the way out, I do not think that there are two institutions in the Universe which contradict each other so flatly as Buddhism and Christianity." The Theravada

Buddhist believes that there is no God or other power that can disrupt the law of cause and effect in ethics or in anything else. The evil action must be paid for, if not in this life then in another life. No appeal to the Heavens, no tears, no bribe, no sacrificial ritual can prevent the evil action from having evil consequences on its perpetrator. Says the Buddhist *Dhammapada,* "Not in the sky, not in the midst of the sea, nor anywhere on earth is there a spot where a man can be freed (from the consequences) of an evil deed." What could be clearer or more specific than that?

Animals must have suffered much from the Christian doctrine that man is made in the image of God and is endowed with an immortal soul. Although man has an animal body and instincts, he has been taught to set himself apart from the rest of creation. The average Christian believes the animal world exists only for his own benefit. Countless animals would have been spared much torture and suffering if only the Gospels had recorded that Jesus showed compassion towards all living creatures and not merely towards mankind. True He spoke admiringly of the shepherd's devotion to his sheep. On the other hand it is told how, in restoring the sanity of a man, He caused a herd of swine to perish in the sea. Possibly this story is untrue—but its effect must have been to spread indifference among Christians to the animal world. The Roman Catholic Church, with its uncompromising anthropomorphism, has officially been too indifferent to animal welfare. Thus the ill-treatment of most beasts of burden in Roman Catholic countries and their backwardness in adopting humane methods of slaughter—if any method of killing can be described as "humane." On the other hand some are now belatedly realizing that Christian love can and should be extended to include the beasts and the birds. Yet in the self-styled "Christian countries" thousands of animals are tortured by vivisectionists, who aim at saving more human life, or decimating the enemy in future wars. And Christians still bait, hunt, and slaughter the loveliest and most noble of non-human creatures in the name of sport or recreation. The cruelty of Christians towards animals is, indeed, only rivalled by that of the Moslems.

"Love animals," wrote Dostoevski, "God has given them the rudiments of thought and joy untroubled. Do not trouble their joy, don't harass them, don't deprive them of their happiness, don't work against God's intent. Man, do not pride yourself on superiority to animals; they are without sin, and you, with your greatness, defile the earth by your appearance on it, and leave the traces of your foulness after you—alas, it is true of almost every one of us!"

Dostoevski, the Russian Orthodox Christian, was talking like a Theravada Buddhist of Thailand, Burma, Ceylon, or Cambodia. Had he visited these countries he would have had the joy of seeing such teaching in practice. He would have met "wild" beasts who were unafraid of man. For the Buddhist can encounter wild life without itching to maim or to kill. In the view of the Buddhist, wilfully to destroy a living thing is to destroy part of oneself. This is because the Buddhist does not see himself as a solitary, separate entity, but part of the universal organism that includes all living things, human and animal. In his conceit and egotism a non-Buddhist may insist upon his separateness. Yet this is just as foolish as claiming that a bubble on a wave isn't part of the ocean. Anyhow, the Buddhist develops a compassion that makes him recoil against causing unnecessary suffering or harm to the lowliest of animals.

The Buddha taught his disciples to extend the spirit of

loving kindness to all living creatures. He forbade the sacrifices of animals. He went to work to get a pension for a royal elephant that was unfit for further labor. Once, while on a preaching tour, the Buddha freed a deer caught in a hunter's trap. Then, sitting under a tree, he sank deep in meditation. The infuriated hunter attempted to shoot him, only to realize his folly and to become another convert to the Buddha's gospel of loving kindness.

As I pondered and argued with myself in Bangkok, I thought also of the innumerable Christian wars, persecutions, and bitter doctrinal quarrels. The awful facts of these had always bewildered me. The Roman Catholic Church claimed to be divinely led and inspired. Yet it had waged bloody wars and had committed unspeakable atrocities in the sacred name of Jesus. The Spanish Inquisition was but one of these terrors, ironically symbolized by the Cross. The persons put to death in this numbered 31,000, according to the Spanish historian Llorente. Earlier, hundreds of thousands died in the fanatical Crusades. The Reformation was a blood bath. It is difficult to decide who were the more barbarous in their fight over Christian dogma, the Catholics or the Protestants. It is still more difficult to believe that these rival religious factions who acted so horribly were faithful believers in the Jesus Christ of the Sermon on the Mount. But in spite of everything, Catholics and Protestants of today claim that through the centuries Christ has revealed himself to the world through their churches.

Buddhists have never waged wars over their religion. There have been no Buddhist inquisitions, or persecutions, or conversions by force, or bloody assaults on devotees of non-Buddhist sects. Buddhism, indeed, has a tolerance and breadth of mind that the squabbling rival churches of Christendom would find hard to understand. The Buddhist must respect every other living person, regardless of his beliefs. To the true Buddhist the life of an enemy is as inviolate as the life of a friend. All violence is therefore evil and must be eschewed. Good should be returned for evil; ill-will must be met by its opposite. Jesus Christ also told men to love their enemies and to do good to those that hate. Organized Christianity, in its warmaking and persecuting, treated such admonitions with flagrant contempt. The Buddhists, on the other hand, were staunchly faithful to their own gospel of peace and non-violence.

All these were my thoughts in Bangkok. And then I had to admit to myself in amazement that I had embraced the 2,500-year-old philosophy of so many Asians. Its immortal freshness and sweetness swept through me. I felt glad and free. I had comprehended. And in my comprehension of Buddhism I came to know the real Christ. I knew that Christianity could be a good and a pure religion if all the theology and superstition were dropped and concentration was made on its teachings of love and forgiveness. And I lost all uncharitableness towards diverse modes of religious expression as I tried increasingly to emulate the tolerance of the Buddha.

1 THE GREATEST MAN

I

"If there is one place on the face of the earth," wrote Romain Rolland, "where all the dreams of living men have found a home from the very earliest days when man began to dream of existence, it is India." The Buddha was a son of India, and he brought fulfillment to a mass of her ancient dreams in the discovery that was to endow life with sense and happiness. The greatest man was born about the year 560 B.C.; and in the same period the philosopher Heraclitus was teaching in Greece. At the time of the Buddha's birth India was not in a Dark Age but in a period of great dreams and exciting intellectual speculation which, alas, were being stifled and discouraged by religious conventionality and by a caste system that was becoming increasingly rigid. The Buddha, through his compelling message and radiant personality, led a peaceful but triumphal revolt against the straitjackets of orthodoxy. That is why he has been described as "a heretic of Hinduism."

The Buddha was an Aryan. That is, he was one of that Sanskrit-speaking race who had poured through the north-west passes into India, probably about 2000 B.C. From these mystical and imaginative Aryans came the Vedas which, even today, are regarded by some Hindus as revealed scripture. In the words of the late Rabindranath Tagore, the Vedas are "a poetic testament of a people's collective reaction to the wonder and awe of existence." They were hymns, poems, and outpourings of the human spirit at the beauty of nature and the miracle of life. But as the Aryan establishment in India developed the class and caste system, and as a priesthood preyed upon the superstitious fears of the masses, the pure and natural messages of the Vedas became distorted. Priests turned the Vedas into "Holy Scriptures," reshaped their naturalness into a complicated cult with which to awe and control the common people. Organized religion thus concentrated on elaborate rites and ceremonies, with cruel and repulsive animal sacrifices; on dreams, omens, and their divination. Previously these Aryan Indians had believed that their Atman, or soul, was one with the soul of the universe. But now this idea of unity between man and all nature was changing into the belief that man was a thing apart and that he possessed a separate, immortal soul.

Despite the growing power of priesthood and convention, however, the impulse towards intellectual activity and bold inquiry became strong. Defying the priests and the caste-consciousness of Brahmanism, large numbers of men (and some women too) would leave their homes for a wandering life of asceticism and meditation. Under trees, in huts and caves, lived hermits who claimed to have penetrated to "the truth." And to them came folk of all ages eager to hear and to weigh various rival teachings. The theory was widespread that asceticism would bring happiness, that the man who starved and inflicted suffering on himself would comprehend spiritual truth and find bliss—if not in this life then in rebirth in successive lives. There was general belief in the transmigration of souls, but this belief differed widely from the Buddha's teaching on rebirth with craving as its cause. Many of the hermits and so-called holy men were of ghastly, repulsive appearance. Some not only starved themselves into living skeletons; they also revelled in being dirty, in consuming indescribable filth as food. Some of the teachers who tramped around the countryside, preaching their competing versions of truth, were adept at subtle argument. Buddhist records ironically describe these professional disputants as "eel wrigglers and hair-splitters."

It was into this religious and philosophic Indian world of convention and eccentricity, of superstition and daring thought, that the prince, who was to become the Buddha, was born. And later he was to sweep away irrelevant contradictions and paralyzing controversy with enduring answers to the problems of mankind. He was to defy the arrogance of the orthodox priesthood, to pour scorn on the importance of caste and on the efficacy of ritualistic and sacrificial practices. And he was to preach a loving kindness and tolerance for all men, animals, and things; a loving kindness with which many Buddhists are radiant even today. However, the founder of Buddhism was born a Hindu and he married a Hindu. He always maintained a belief in some of the purer Hindu doctrines. But the Buddha's philosophy that he taught took the form of a practical program to help ordinary men and women through the journey of life. Many Hindus now admit a great debt to the Buddha because the influence of his teachings has done so much to improve Hinduism. Said the saintly Mahatma Gandhi: "It is my deliberate opinion that the essential part of the teaching of the Buddha now forms an integral part of Hinduism. The Buddha never rejected Hinduism, but he broadened its basis and gave it a new life and a new interpretation."

The Buddha was a man—not a god. He died as we all must die, and he had no resurrection. Legend, superstition, and wishful thinking have created biographies of the Buddha filled with stories of the miraculous. As in the case of Jesus, his authentic record has been smothered in pious but fantastic fiction. We are told that his body hurtled through space; how flowers descended upon him from Heaven; and how his presence attracted soft, lovely music and sweet scents from nowhere. But the Buddha performed at least one miracle that has been fully authenticated. He produced an explanation of life and a solution to its problems that have, through the centuries, been a sure guide to hundreds of millions of men and women. These teachings, with their strictly rational background, have survived the centuries; they are being hailed as those of a genius by Western scientists, philosophers, and psychologists. H. G. Wells in his *Outline of History* placed the Buddha as first among the greatest men who ever lived. Two thousand five hundred years ago the Buddha made statements that today's physicists are proving. The striking parallel between Buddhist theories and those of modern physics has been convincingly stressed by the French author Maurice Percheron, who comments, "And so we see physics joining Buddhism in its theory of universal flux, of lack of substance inherent in matter, of impermanence, of fundamental error attaching to the testimony of the senses and consequently of doubt over the validity of the mind's speculations."

The greatest man was born 100 miles northeast of Benares. His father Suddhodana Gotama was chief or Rajah of the Sakyas, an Aryan tribe at Kapilavatthu on the banks of the Rohini River. The domain of Suddhodana was on the borders of modern Nepal. From it were breathtaking views of the Himalayas, majestic and mysterious. The Sakyas made their living by farming. Although Suddhodana's country was tiny by modern standards, he and his family were wealthy and lived in luxury. Rajah Suddhodana had two wives who were sisters, the daughters of the chief of a neighboring tribe, the Koliyans. For many years the two women were childless. When Maya, the elder wife, was forty-five she told her husband she was going to have a baby. As the time of birth drew near a custom of that age decreed that wives go to the homes of their parents for confinement. So Maya left her husband's palace and, with a retinue of attendants, started for the house of her father and mother miles away. The party reached a park known as Lumbini, with groves of fine trees, when Maya's labor pains began. Her child—a son—was born under the trees. Mother, baby, and attendants returned to the palace of her husband. Maya was very ill—and within a week she was dead. The thriving baby was placed under the care of Maya's devoted sister, Pajapati.

The little prince was given the first name of Siddhattha and he inherited the family name of Gotama. But he was to become known and beloved through centuries by countless millions as the Buddha (the Enlightened or Awakened One), as the Tathagata (Well-Arrived) and other exalted titles. The motherless prince grew into a youth of great physical beauty and magnetic charm. He had bold athletic prowess, but also a supersensitiveness that in youth is rare. In adulthood meditation the Buddha was to recall a boyhood occasion of this sensitiveness. It was springtime. Prince

Siddhattha's father, as ruler, was taking part in a ceremonial celebration of spring ploughing and sowing. The rajah strode through a field turning the soil with a jewelled plough. The boy Siddhattha watched. This was a festive occasion—but the boy saw only sadness. His eyes were not on his richly dressed father or the ornate plough but on the worms and insects that it brought to the surface from the brown earth. He saw the birds descend to devour the insects in their powerlessness. Of infinite compassion, Siddhattha was sorry for the worms and the insects. But in this sight too his mind comprehended the cruel remorselessness of nature and life. This, in miniature, was the inescapable pain and suffering of the world.

Boyhood had scarcely passed when Siddhattha married. Legend has endowed his bride, Gopa Yasodhara, with exquisite beauty and every virtue. Legend also says he won her in a contest of arms. However, it is more likely that, in keeping with Hindu tradition, the marriage was arranged by the young couple's parents and that they never saw one another until the wedding ceremony. Yasodhara, daughter of the Rajah of Koli, was, indeed, a cousin of Siddhattha. It seems that this was a dynastic marriage; and it was successful, until that fateful day in world history when Siddhattha abandoned all to seek spiritual enlightenment.

India has a history of mysticism so ancient that its genesis cannot be traced. She also has a record of sensuality that is probably just as old. Prince Siddhattha delighted in the pleasures of sense lavishly offered to a personage of his class. He had three palaces—one for summer, one for winter and one for the rainy season. There were the usual royal musicians, the corps of shapely dancing girls, the rich foods, the sensuous art, and the sport. The doting father, the

Rajah Suddhodana, contrived to keep worry and sorrow from Siddhattha, to isolate him from the hard outside world by encouraging him to limit his interests to the gilded luxuries and pastimes of the palaces. However, within a few years such pleasures began to cloy. An unbidden guest in the palace revels—sensed only by the young prince—was the skeleton of sorrow, suffering, and death. Siddhattha became a difficult, brooding person; restless and unhappy. Rebelliously he would leave his palaces to be driven into the city with Channa, his charioteer and friend. In the course of these chariot trips into teeming Kapilavatthu, Siddhattha would have seen thousands of persons, from the well-fed rich to the starving beggars. But three particular individuals and one corpse specially attracted his attention, making an indelible impression upon his mind. These three men and the corpse stirred the mental crisis and revolt that led the prince to desert forever the little country that one day he would have ruled.

The first sight to worry Siddhattha in Kapilavatthu was an emaciated, tottering, toothless man in his eighties laboriously trying to make his way through the jostling crowds. Painfully touched by the pathos of the old fellow, the prince turned sadly to this charioteer Channa and blurted, "What man is this?" Channa, brief but realistic, replied, "This comes to all men." The second sight was a sick man with black plague of the groin. He was a repulsive-looking person, and crying from his intense pains. The third was a decaying corpse being carried by heart-broken relatives to the funeral pyre. And on these second and third sights too the prince despairingly questioned Channa, only to hear him repeat again, "This comes to all men."

The fourth and final sight before Siddhattha's great decision came at a time of national and household excitement. The prince was twenty-nine. He had been married more than ten years. Yet Yasodhara had not borne a child. Now at last a baby was expected. The loyal Sakya populace impatiently awaited the arrival, prayed it would be a boy and prepared gay celebrations. Again Siddhattha was chariot riding with Channa. He was attracted by a slim, barefooted man with a shaven head. The man wore a tattered yellow robe. Once more the pondering prince turned to Channa with the question, "What man is this?" Doubtless Siddhattha recognized this man as a wandering religious ascetic. But who does not, when specially stirred, ask a close friend obvious questions? Channa replied that the wanderer was "One who has gone forth to the homeless life." Siddhattha looked at the ragged, penniless wanderer and envied him. Siddhattha was endowed with what the world would call "everything." He was handsome, healthy, aristocratic, and with great possessions. He had a loving wife who was soon to present him with a child. Nevertheless he despised these so-called blessings because so many others in the world seemed, not only unblessed, but cursed. Now Siddhattha had sufficient glimpses into the tragedy of sickness, want, old age, and death to be unable to wallow selfishly in his own good fortune. And he realized that this was transitory anyway. Not even princes can command or buy themselves out of sickness, bodily decay, and dissolution. Siddhattha saw that this wandering ascetic possessed most because he possessed nothing. He was free of all material and family entanglements. He could without interruption, and without wasting effort on the satisfaction of physical yearnings, meditate with concentration upon the mystery of life and its suffering. If there was a solution to the desperate plight of mankind, then such a man would have the best chance of finding it.

Later the Buddha was to tell his followers of the thoughts that led him to renounce all and join the yellow-robed homeless wanderers:

"There is a getting born and a growing old, a dying and being reborn. And from this suffering, alas! an escape is not known, even from old age and death. How shall such escape be found? Surely there must be a way out of this mass of ill? Just as there is warmth as opposed to cold, and light as against darkness, there must likewise be happiness as opposed to sorrow?

"There was a time when I, too, valued only things that must change and die in time. But the thought came to me, 'Why should I not pursue, instead, the happiness of the holy life which transcends this life of sorrow?' There came a time when I, while quite young, with a wealth of jet-black hair, and in all the beauty of early manhood, cut off my hair and beard, put on the orange robe and went out from home to homelessness."

The old man . . . the sick man . . . the decaying corpse . . . the homeless ascetic. These four sights, haunting Siddhattha's mind, brought him to the eve of the Great Renunciation, as Buddhists call it. After seeing the ascetic and being so deeply stirred, the prince went into a garden on the riverside. Now he had decided to abandon all in order to go forth into the countryside in supreme quest for the answer to the enigma of mankind's pain and sorrow. But first he would have to face the agonies of breaking the ties with those he loved and who loved him. He would have to desert his wife, who was so devoted and so lovely; leave his father and aunt and dash to the dust all the ambitions they cherished for him; renounce the throne to which he was heir; and turn his back upon a fine and loyal people. Suddenly officials came running to Siddhattha in the garden. Joyfully they told him that his princess, Yasodhara, had just given birth to a son, unexpectedly early. The response of the prince to the news astonished them. Quietly he said, "This is a new and strong tie I shall have to break." He re-entered Kapilavatthu to find himself wildly welcomed by the crowds, rejoicing that the rajah at last had a grandson. The song of one young girl, rising above the din, made Siddhattha ponder. She sang:

Happy indeed is the Mother,
Happy indeed is the Father,
Happy indeed is the Wife,
Who has such a Husband.

In their language, the word "happy" had a second meaning. This other meaning was "freed." So the girl's song pleased Siddhattha, since he interpreted it as meaning that, in renouncing the material world, he would free mankind from pain and endless rebirth. Removing his necklace of pearls he gave it to the astonished girl. She mistook this gesture for one of romantic courtship. She failed to comprehend that her simple verse was, in his ears, an inspiring hymn.

At midnight the first chapter of the Buddha's 80-year life ended. Religious history offers no scene more poignant. The prince ordered Channa to get his horse Kanthaka. Then he entered the palace room where Yasodhara lay sleeping with the baby on her breast. Gazing upon them in the flickering light, the prince moved to pick up the baby, to fondle him for the first and last time. But to touch the baby would have meant awaking Yasodhara; so the prince looked at them for several moments, then slipped silently from the room. Elsewhere he gazed on the palace's sleeping dancing girls. So attractive when they were awake and decked for his entertainment, the girls were in their slumber sprawled in unlovely attitudes. Their faces, sweet in wakefulness, now were dull and lifeless. Siddhattha was momentarily repulsed by the scene. Repulsion turned quickly into compassion for these dancing girls. Who, in watching another in the mystery of sleep, has not been filled with a sadness? Siddhattha met Channa outside the palace. They rode together in the moonlight to the forest and dismounted. Siddhattha drew his small sharp sword and slashed off his long black hair. This was but one of many acts of renunciation for long hair was a symbol of nobility among the Sakyas. Next Siddhattha took off his necklace and bejewelled ornaments and gave them to Channa. Now he asked his friend to return to the palace, taking the horse Kanthaka with him. Channa begged to remain with the prince, offering to share in a life of homelessness and asceticism. But the prince replied, "You must go—or how will my father and others know what has become of me?"

Critics have condemned Siddhattha for his manner of leaving home and country. One Christian described it to me as "callous abandonment of wife and family." Yet what would have happened if he had not left so stealthily, if he had approached his loved ones for a formal farewell? They would, of course, have implored him to change his mind. The scenes would have been hysterical, and quite possibly the little domain of the Rajah Suddhodana would have been thrown into turmoil. Then probably Siddhattha dared not tell his father and wife his renunciation plans lest they should successfully persuade him to abandon them. Siddhattha was a full-blooded young man in the prime of life. As it was, the temptation not to abandon all in order to seek the truth must have been tremendous. When in his final moments in the palace he looked at his slumbering wife and their newborn son, resistance to the impulse to remain must have caused him agony. Certainly in those days in India it was considered a noble thing for a man to forsake home and loved ones to become an ascetic and a hermit. However, consider the shock it would cause in Britain if the heir to the throne on reaching manhood insisted upon becoming an Anglican monk. All things considered, it would seem that Siddhattha was right in boldly and quickly achieving his plan through a *fait accompli.*

Alone at last, Siddhattha walked on through the wilds to the city of Rajagaha in the territory of powerful King Bimbisara. He had longed for the life of a mendicant. Now he came to know this in its less romantic reality, as for the first time the prince started begging from door to door. He was disgusted by the sight of the sticky mess of food scraps that the housewives gave him. This fastidious young man—accustomed to the delicacies of a palace dining-table—was even tempted by his nausea to abandon his truth-seeking mission. "Am I to give up my quest by such trivial considerations as the quality of food?" he pondered. "At least such food will keep my body alive and help me to pursue my search." And never again was he fussy about his diet.

A number of hermits lived in caves in the hills that surrounded Rajagaha. Among them were two religious teachers named Alara Kalama and Udraka Ramaputra. Siddhattha went first to Alara and then to Udraka to study their systems of self-discipline and penance which, they claimed, would give a man insight into the mystery of existence and endow him with superhuman powers. But the instruction of Alara and Udraka was not enough. He felt he must test to the full the usefulness of penance to win the mental and physical purity that might help him to apprehend truth. In this mood of extreme self-mortification Siddhattha plunged into the jungles in the neighborhood of the present temple of Buddha Gaya. He had attracted five disciples of asceticism. They were Kondanna, Bhaddiya, Vappa, Mahanama, and Assaji. Siddhattha's experiment lasted six years: it ended in failure. In later life he was to give a horrible description of the tortures he inflicted upon himself during those years. In experiments fanatical in their extremity, he would stop himself breathing. "Then did dreadful pains come into my head. Just as if a strong man were twisting a stout leathern thong around my head, thus did violent pains assail my head." He starved himself "until my body reached a state of utter exhaustion. Just as the rafters of a tottering house fall this way and that, so did my ribs fall this way and that from lack of sustenance. Just as in a deep, deep well the sparkle of the waters may be seen sunk in the depths below, so in the depths of their sockets did the lustre of my eyes seem sunk through the same lack of sustenance." With the mind weakened by such self-torture Siddhattha lost instead of gained the power to think with clarity.

One day the human skeleton staggered and fell. Some thought he was dead. On regaining consciousness Siddhattha realized the folly of severe self-mortification. In the words of the Buddhists' beloved *Dhammapada,* "Not nakedness, nor matted hair, nor dust and dirt, nor sleeping on bare floors, nor squatting on the heels can purify a man who has not solved his doubts. But one who, though beautifully dressed, has a mind that is powerful and restrained, who is chaste and who has abandoned all harm to human beings—he is indeed a Brahmin, ascetic, and monk." Now Siddhattha took a sensible meal of nourishing rice gruel and decided to starve himself no more. But Siddhattha's five ascetic friends were horrified and disillusioned. "As soon as I started taking substantial meals those five brethren went away, saying 'Gotama, the recluse, has become luxurious. He wavers in his purpose. He has retreated to the luxurious life.' " The five deserted Siddhattha. They left the forest for the sacred city of Benares.

Siddhattha wandered on into the neighborhood of Uruvela on the banks of the Neranjara River. There he "beheld a lovely spot, a pleasant forest grove with a river of clear water flowing by, easy of access and delightful." Sujata, the daughter of a villager, brought him a bowl of curds. After eating, he washed himself. Then he sat under a Bodhi-tree and vowed, "Let my skin, sinews, and bones shrivel and wither; let my flesh and blood dry up. I will not stir from this seat until I have obtained absolute insight." So under the Bodhi-tree this one emaciated man in his shoddy yellow robe fought the most momentous battle in history. The results of this battle have affected the outlook and moulded the characters of millions and millions of men and women from that day to this. Asia would have been and would be a different place today had not Siddhattha's meditative struggle under that tree won him the knowledge for a religion or philosophy that has guided these masses of persons in their hard pilgrimage from birth to death. What would Asia have become had not Siddhattha won his battle for enlightenment? There is little doubt but that without the inspiration of his teachings vast areas of that continent would have been dominated by ungoverned hatreds, lusts, and selfish desires. Of course these have often been rampant. But at the same time they have been prevented from lasting triumph by masses of sweet, kindly folk softened and purified by the teachings of Prince Siddhattha who, in his victory under the Bodhi-tree, became the Buddha.

As Siddhattha settled under the tree he was first tortured by a sense of failure and loneliness. His six years of self-mortification had been a fiasco. The five disciples had abandoned him in anger. Now he was alone, except for enticing memories of the princely life that he had, in his youthful religious zeal, repudiated. Into his fevered imagination came pictures of the delights still offered him, if he would only grasp them and forget this quest for philosophical truth. He recalled the intoxicating joys of love and sex, the thrills of power, the relaxation of wealth and luxury. In the imagery of his time he saw in his imagination Mara, the tempter and evil one, inviting him back to the old life. He saw, too, in his dreamlike meditation his wife Yasodhara, in all her exquisiteness, beckoning him home. Yet those tempting mental pictures failed to black out Siddhattha's realization of the impermanence and unreality of human life. Joy was never truly grasped. It was offered; then snatched away by torturing time. Life tantalized, but never satisfied. And through it all ran the black river of pain and sorrow, sooner or later engulfing all living creatures. The temptation to return to his old life passed, never to come back. Under that tree his concentration became more intense. Siddhattha recalled his past lives, he contemplated the universe and its conditions and pondered over the intricacies of cause and effect. Then, in the words of an English Buddhist monk, Bhikkhu Mahinda, "The vast panorama of life and philosophy fell, like interlocking pieces of a jig-saw puzzle, into one complete whole. He had realized Truth and the exact nature of Reality, and the Dhamma or Law of Life became known by man for the deliverance of mankind."

At last the long strivings and self-sacrifice and meditation of Siddhattha had triumphed. He had attained supreme enlightenment. He had become the Buddha, the Enlightened One. Joyously he ended his struggle for the Light with this song of victory: [1]

Many a house of life
Hath held me—seeking ever him who wrought
These prisons of the senses, sorrow-fraught;
Sore was my ceaseless strife!
But now,
Thou builder of this Tabernacle—Thou!
I know Thee! Never shalt Thou build again
These walls of pain,
Nor raise the roof-tree of deceits, nor lay
Fresh rafters on the clay;
Broken Thy house is, and the ridge-pole split!
Delusion fashioned it!
Safe pass I thence—deliverance to obtain.

The man who had discovered the secret of happiness was for some time undecided whether he should keep it to himself or share it with others. The formula was simple, although the theory behind it was abstruse. The Buddha doubted whether his doctrine was not too coldly plain and matter-of-fact for excitable, superstitious mankind. The doctrine offered no benevolent god, no magic-working priests, no ceremonies or sacrifices of propitiation. It did not claim that God was a man or that Man was a god. However, the

[1] Sir Edwin Arnold, *The Light of Asia.*

Buddha had always loved his fellow men and felt part of them. Indeed, it was his compassion for the suffering ones he saw in Kapilavatthu that made him abandon all to seek the cure of suffering. So how could the Buddha save himself without also saving others? At least some people would grasp his message. Thus the Enlightened One banished his hesitation and decided to tell anyone who would listen about his great discovery. He thought of the five mendicant brethren who had shared his six years of experiment in asceticism: Kondanna, Bhaddiya, Vappa, Mahanama, and Assaji. True that they had turned their backs on him for abandoning extreme asceticism. Nevertheless the Buddha wanted them to be the first to hear the details of his enlightenment. Therefore he turned towards Benares where he knew the five had gone. On the way to Benares the Buddha met an old acquaintance named Upaka, who was a member of a naked sect. Upaka noticed a remarkable change in the man he had known as Gotama. "How is it," he asked, "that your form is so perfect, your face so lovely and your appearance so peaceful? What religion is it that gives you such joy and peace?" The reply of Gotama was that he had no teacher but that he was himself the Absolute Buddha, the conqueror of ignorance, sin, and desire. "I am going to Benares," added Gotama, "to set in motion the wheel of the excellent doctrine." Upaka was skeptical, and we can understand his feeling that such enormous claims, made so suddenly, were extravagant. "It may be so, friend," commented Upaka, walking off the opposite way.

The Buddha found his five former disciples in the deer park of Sarnath, a few miles north of Benares. When the disciples saw him approaching they quickly resolved to meet him with a snub. They planned not to rise to greet him or to offer him refreshment. The Buddha came closer—obviously now a radiant figure who compelled respect. Then the five arose—despite their plan—and offered to wash his feet as well as other courtesies. However, they addressed him as "friend"—not a very respectful term. He rebuked them for this, announced himself as the Buddha and offered to show them an escape from the evils of existence. The five were the audience of the Buddha's first sermon. This outlined the basis of his entire doctrine. It explained the Middle Way, the Four Noble Truths, and the Noble Eightfold Path. The Middle Way, leading to serenity and wisdom, avoided the two extremes of uncontrolled satisfaction of the senses and fanatical austerity or asceticism. It was a path of sane moderation. The Four Noble Truths boldly recognized the fact of suffering; that suffering was caused by the craving for personal satisfaction; that suffering would end when such craving ceased; and that this could be accomplished through the Noble Eightfold Path. This way of life consisted of right view, right resolution, right speech, right conduct, right livelihood, right effort, right mindfulness, right concentration. These simple yet deeply profound truths will be thoroughly discussed in a later chapter. Their effect upon Kondanna, eldest of the five ascetics, was immediate and he became one of the Buddha's first converts. Soon the other four became the Buddha's disciples too. Another early disciple was a rich young man named Yasa. Unbalanced by the cares of the world Yasa had been wandering in crazed distraction when he found the Buddha and peace. Yasa's mother and former wife became the Buddha's first women lay followers.

In the deer park at Sarnath the number of the Buddha's followers grew to sixty. He sent them in all directions as missionaries of the new gospel. "In the spirit and in the letter," he told them, "make ye known the perfect, utterly pure, righteous life." Later he taught them a simple ceremony for the initiation of converts. The words for converts to repeat were the same as those repeated by all Buddhists today:

> *I take my refuge in the Buddha,*
> *I take my refuge in the Dhamma (Teaching),*
> *I take my refuge in the Sangha (Order).*

From the deer park he went into the wilds. There he found a sect of fire worshippers led by Uruvela Kassapa. Appropriately he preached them a sermon on fires. He discussed three disruptive human fires: greed, hatred, and illusion. These are little Hells that man carries around with him until he quenches them and thus finds peace.

Kassapa and all his followers joined the Buddha. They accompanied him and his other disciples in the walk to Rajagaha in the country of King Bimbisara. This is where the Buddha had first come more than six years before after renouncing the princely life and its luxuries. Here he had wandered as a shy novice in beggary, revolted by the messy scraps that were slopped into his bowl. Few in Rajagaha had heard of Siddhattha. Now, as the Buddha, he was returning to a Rajagaha where even the king awaited his arrival with interest; for already the news of his extraordinary Benares sermons and their results had reached Bimbisara's country. King and subjects also heard he was now on his way with a company of disciples and converts. They welcomed him into Rajagaha; but they were surprised to see that Kassapa was a member of the party. Kassapa, who for years had sacrificed to Agni, the fire god, astonished the crowd by prostrating himself at the Buddha's feet, by denouncing sacrificial rites and by asserting that men governed by their passions would never find peace. Soon King Bimbisara and many of his people embraced the new philosophy. Bimbisara presented the Buddha with a park known as the Bamboo Grove as a retreat for him and his monks.

It was in the Bamboo Grove that the Buddha converted Sariputta and Moggallana, who were to become two of his most brilliant disciples and missionaries. Many writers on Buddhism, even in this twentieth century, have remarked upon the beautiful and serene countenances of truly dedicated Buddhists. Thus, in those very early days, Sariputta was impressed by the countenance of Assaji, one of the five ascetics who had abandoned the Buddha, only to join him again as converts in the deer park at Sarnath. Sariputta asked Assaji the name of his teacher. And Assaji replied, giving the essence of the Buddha's teaching in this massive brevity:

Of all things that proceed from a cause,
The Buddha has stated the cause
And also explained their ceasing.
This the great sage has proclaimed.

Soon afterwards Sariputta and his friend Moggallana were welcomed by the Buddha into the Order.

II

Into a grove outside Kapilavatthu moved a weary and dusty company of monks. Their leader was Prince Siddhattha, now the Buddha, who on a moonlit night years previously had crept from his palace and ridden into the wilds on the start of his long, agonizing search for enlightenment. Now, on the entreaties of his father, the Rajah Suddhodana, he was returning home for a visit. The news spread from the grove to Kapilavatthu that Siddhattha—once so beloved by its people—was back. Suddhodana, with his brothers and attendants, hastened towards the grove to bid Siddhattha welcome. This was, in the father's eyes, the return of the prodigal; and the father was ready to "forgive." Suddhodana and company reached the grove. He searched for the son he had once loved, with long jet-black hair, expensively dressed and bejewelled. Instead he found a weatherbeaten, hairless Siddhattha, in tattered yellow robe, surrounded by a monkish riff-raff. According to accepted rules of courtesy Suddhodana should have welcomed Siddhattha and his companions and offered them food. Instead he offered them nothing, and hurried away. Next day Siddhattha annoyed his father still more by leaving the grove and wandering about Kapilavatthu begging for food. Suddhodana found the mendicant prince and candidly expressed his embarrassment at his behavior. He led his son back to the palace where, in spite of everything, a royal assemblage greeted him with respect and honor. He looked at their faces. Yasodhara, his wife, was not there. She was in her own palace with Rahula their son. And she was saying, "If I mean anything at all to my husband he will come to me here." He did come soon afterwards, with two of his yellow-robed followers. Yasodhara took one look at her husband who had become the Buddha and fell at his feet in tears. Later she sent a brightly dressed Rahula to his father to demand his rights and inheritance as son of a Sakya prince. "I'm so happy to be near you, father," were the boy's first words on approaching him. Rahula followed the Buddha demanding, "Give me my inheritance." The Buddha's answer was to ask the disciple Sariputta to receive Rahula as a member of the Order. This was another hard blow to Suddhodana, the boy's grandfather. Suddhodana implored the Buddha that thenceforth no minor should be admitted to the Order without his parents' consent. The Buddha agreed that this should become the rule. But Rahula remained a monk; and when an Order for female mendicants was established, one of its first members was Yasodhara.

Again the Buddha left his home country, returning to Rajagaha. His Order was growing fast. More rulers were supporting his work. Rich merchants and their wives were financing many new retreats for his monks. The message of the Buddha was spreading over many hundreds of miles of northeast India. Wherever he went there were large curious crowds and new converts. Two cousins had joined the Buddha's community, Ananda and Devadatta. Ananda became the Buddha's personal attendant. He was an attractive, fallible person with weaknesses he found hard to conquer. Ananda's affection for the Buddha was deep. Some of the Buddha's loveliest observations on life and conduct were made to Ananda. Devadatta had none of Ananda's simple loyalty and affection. He could be compared to a plotting ecclesiastic of Europe's Middle Ages. His was a jealous, ambitious, scheming nature. He plotted against the Buddha with the intention of replacing him as chief of the Order. He even succeeded in winning the support of Ajatasattu, son of King Bimbisara, against the Buddha. Several murder attempts were planned by Devadatta—but all in vain. When Devadatta arranged for some hired assassins to kill the Buddha, they became his devoted converts. When Devadatta loosed a ferocious elephant in the Buddha's path, it became docile and friendly. Devadatta formed a rival Order to the Buddha's—but this collapsed.

The Buddha died at the age of eighty after forty-five

years as the Enlightened One. Of his last resting places in these years of wandering, one was on property given to his Order by Ambapali, a prostitute. Ambapali had come to him while he was visiting the town of Vaisali, eager to hear his message. This wealthy courtesan invited him to her mansion to dinner and he accepted. The Licchavi, a princely family of Vaisali, were astounded when Ambapali told them of the Buddha's acceptance of her hospitality. They tried to bribe her to let them become the hosts instead. Next they tried to make the Buddha cancel his engagement with Ambapali in order to dine with them. The Buddha refused, and, throwing up their hands, members of the aristocratic Licchavis complained, "A woman of the world has outdone us! We have been left behind by a frivolous girl!" After the dinner the reformed prostitute sat on a low stool at the Buddha's side. And the records tell how "the Blessed One instructed, roused, and gladdened her with religious edification." She gave him her mango grove. He moved on to another place. Illness struck him and he realized that, at last, death was nearing. He told Ananda:

"I am grown old and full of years; my journey is drawing to a close. Be ye refuges and islands unto yourselves."

Here was a call that has inspired adherents of Buddhism throughout its long history. And who, reflecting on these words of the Enlightened One, would dare to repeat the monstrous and widely-spread criticism that Buddhism is a religion for weaklings and defeatists? He said frankly he would die and not return. He told of no loving Heavenly Father who would save man from the folly of his sins. Man, in the Buddha's view, would have to be very staunch and very brave. For only man could save himself—unaided.

The Buddha threw off his illness—but not for long. Moving to Pava he was entertained at a meal of rice and pork by a goldsmith named Cunda. The same day he started for the village of Kusinara. On the way he fell desperately ill and rested on the riverside under a sal tree. Later he noticed that Ananda was no longer among the monks around him. Ananda was found weeping and saying, "The master, who is so kind, is about to pass away from me!" He was led to the dying Buddha, who begged him not to weep.

"Have I not already told you," he said to Ananda, "that it is in the very nature of things, most near and dear to us, that we must separate from them and leave them? For a long time, Ananda, you have been very near to me through thoughts and acts of love beyond all measure. You have done well, Ananda. Be earnest in effort and you will soon be free from the great evils—from sensuality, from individuality, from delusion, and from ignorance."

Families came out from Kusinara to the grove where the Buddha now lay. And in those final hours he made his last convert—a wanderer named Subhadda. Subhadda received the dying man's teaching with cries of "Wonderful, Oh Lord! A marvel, Oh Lord!" The Buddha asked his monks if there was any doubt or perplexity concerning his teaching that he could clarify before he passed on. "Don't," he warned, "be remorseful in the future at the thought, 'We had not the heart to question the Exalted One, though we were in his very presence.'" Ananda assured him that the brethren had not a single doubt or perplexity concerning the Buddha, the Order, and the Path to Enlightenment.

Then came the Buddha's dying words: "Decay is inherent in all component things! Work out your salvation with diligence!"

When he lost consciousness and passed away, brethren

who still lacked self-discipline threw out their arms and wept, crying, "Too soon has the Blessed One died! Too soon has the Happy One passed from existence! Too soon has the Light of the World gone out!"

"That's enough, brothers," said Anuruddha, a wise and beloved member of the Order. "Don't weep or lament. Didn't the Blessed One tell us that it's in the very nature of things near and dear to us that we must separate from and leave them? For everything that is born contains within itself the inherent necessity of dissolution. How then would it be possible for the body of our Master not to be dissolved? Those who are free from passion will bear the loss, calm and self-possessed, mindful of the truth he has taught us."

Thus spoke a brave man among brave brethren.

2 THE TRUTHS AND THE PATH

The dying Buddha told his listeners to work out their salvation with diligence. And salvation must rationally be based on the Four Noble Truths. We shall now review these in more detail. Christians talk about the "mystery" of suffering. It is no mystery to the Buddhist. He believes that suffering is caused by craving that can never be satisfied. In his ignorance the non-Buddhist is like a baby who cries because he can't be given the moon. The non-Buddhist won't resign himself to the fact that it is impossible to have the moon. He knows that death is inevitable, and that old age is inevitable if he survives youth and middle-age. Yet he is scared by these inescapable facts. Thus he craves eternal life and is disturbed by uncertainty whether or not he has an immortal soul. He is fearsome of natural calamities, accident, and sudden death. The dread always haunts him that something or other might wipe out the bundle of cravings that constitute himself. Life is surely to most people a capsule of pleasure wrapped in an abundance of pain. The joy of procreation results in the pain of birth; the baby in his turn will struggle in the treacherous seas of accident, disease, decay, bereavement, and the tortures of unsatisfied desire. This craving, this insistent demand for self-satisfaction can lead from pain to pain, such as disappointment in love, frustrated ambition, ill-health through drunkenness or gluttony. Craving or greed for wealth and so-called success and sensual satisfaction can, in its desperation, create anger, ill-will, meanness, and evil actions. What is the modern world but a free competition of rival cravings and greeds? And the irony of it all is that the nations and persons popularly regarded as the most successful are also the least lovely.

Despising spurious optimism, the Buddhist therefore follows his reasoning until he accepts the First Noble Truth concerning suffering. He recognizes suffering as universal. Next he grasps the reason for the existence of suffering—desire. This desire is what gives all creation the passionate will to live and expand. Mankind knows the desire not merely to live, but to possess, to win, and to keep; to satiate and pamper the body with so-called pleasures, to feel important and immortal. Such selfish adoration of self breeds misery. However, all men cannot be blamed for creating such misery for themselves. They are ignorant and misled, particularly in these modern times, when material wealth and power are the accepted standards for the success of a nation or a person. The Buddhist knows through the Third Noble Truth that when all these greeds and thirsts are overcome, suffering will decline. Furthermore, through the Buddha's doctrine of rebirth and its causes, the enlightened follower sees how life can in its tragic human form be translated into the state known as Nibbana—but we shall discuss this later. Then, in the Fourth Noble Truth the Buddhist sees how the cravings and lusts of life can be destroyed and happiness attained. Salvation is found on the Noble Eightfold Path.

"Enter on this path and make an end to sorrow," said the Buddha. And his practical system of self-reform, if faithfully followed, does indeed produce a remarkable change in a man's feelings and outlook. It is not a path for monks only. Laymen tread it by the thousands in Ceylon, Burma, Thailand, Cambodia, and elsewhere. Many have told me of the transformation it has wrought in them. One Thai, in a high official position, confided how, after years of indifference to Buddhism and every other religion, he started reading the teachings of the Buddha while ill in hospital. At first sight he thought the Eightfold Path was "paved with platitudes." But experimentally he started to follow it. The first results were so surprising that he persevered in the alert self-discipline it demands. "I had," he added, "been a miserable mixed-up person since my boyhood. Within a year of entering the Path I had become a new man. I didn't get mental and spiritual serenity only. I became more energetic and more awake to everything and everybody around me. Furthermore, my health, which had been poor for years, became perfect." My friend stressed that the Path is no cheap psychological formula to fool a weak, disturbed man into a false sense of well-being. It is a hard system of self-discipline that evades no realities. It offers no divine aid. The person who follows the system must achieve success without any outside help whatsoever. The fact that each individual must work out his own salvation cannot be too strongly emphasized. For the Buddha said: "By oneself alone is evil done, by oneself is one defiled. By oneself is evil avoided, by oneself alone is one purified. Purity and impurity depend on oneself; no one can purify another."

Now for the signposts of the Eightfold Path and their meaning:

RIGHT VIEW

The pilgrim on the Path is expected to look about without rose-colored glasses. He must study the Four Noble Truths without bias and seek their acceptance on the basis of his own reasoning. He must say good-bye to superstition, wishful thinking, and delusion. This is not easy. The pilgrim will realize that in the past his existence was cushioned by false beliefs from false religions and philosophies. He may have leaned mentally on alleged benevolent deities and saints. He may have embraced the still widely disseminated illusion that "All is for the best in this best of all possible worlds" or that "Every cloud has a silver lining." Buddhism has no room for intellectual sissies. It offers no salvation by faith; only by fearless, realistic reasoning and effort. One of the favorite quotations of earnest Buddhists is, "Warriors, warriors, we call ourselves, we fight for splendid virtue, for high endeavor, for sublime wisdom." That is why Right View is so necessary.

RIGHT RESOLUTION

In the words of the Buddha, he who aims at Right Resolution dedicates himself to "renunciation, non-resentment and harmlessness." This must surely begin with a revaluation of values. The pilgrim has probably been a seeker after importance in the worldly sense. He has been proud of his professional or business position. He has thought the pursuit of money to be important. He has been fussily conscious of his appearance and the impression he makes upon other people. Appetites have assumed ridiculous importance. He has been particular about his food, thirsty for stimulating drinks, always craving another cigarette. Satisfaction of the sexual instinct has seemed so important that often it has crowded all other thoughts from the mind. The Buddhist layman is not expected to live with the strictness of the Buddhist monk. He dwells in the workaday world and cannot isolate himself from it. Nevertheless he does not have to accept the workaday world's shoddy values. Thus the layman repudiates them, and no longer gets worried and excited about his professional position, his wealth, his appetites, and cravings. The old motivations are renounced for the Buddhist ideals of simplicity and self-denial. He starts to base his life on the important fact that he is not important. The sense of one's unimportance should help to make the resolution concerning non-resentment easier. It is pride that makes so many people burn with resentment at insult, real or imaginary. It is pride that inspires ill-feeling at another's success. When a man reaches the belief that "I don't really matter," he is not going to be overwhelmed with bitterness at unfairness, insult, or airs of superiority shown him by others. He will also lose feelings of resentment against others, because he will understand how insignificant are all men. Indeed no alleged enemy or rival is worthy of anger or spleen. Psychologists have said that a big proportion of our nervous energy is squandered on resentment and hatred —and these are the parents of the modern "nervous breakdown." The pilgrim of the Eightfold Path must also resolve to do no harm to any sentient being. No true Buddhist would add to the world's misery by wilfully making another person unhappy or by the purposeless killing of an animal. His is a creed of peace, of non-violence. He is not merely a friend of his friend. He is also a friend of his enemy.

RIGHT SPEECH

"What, brethren, is Right Speech?" said the Buddha. "It is abstinence from lying speech, from backbiting and abusive speech, and from idle babble. That, brethren, is called Right Speech." Certainly a liar is out of place in Buddhism, the most honest of the world's major religions. Buddhism, in its Theravadin purity, says a man need accept only the teachings that seem reasonable to him. There are no creeds, and no demands for the unqualified acceptance of dogma. No condemnation in this world or the next awaits the man who conscientiously examines the Buddha's teachings and then says, "I don't believe them." Buddhism has never known such horrors as the burning of Bruno and the slaughter of Hypatia for expressing their honest thoughts. "Faith is the belief in things known to be untrue," wrote cynical Samuel Butler. But in Buddhism nothing has to be accepted on faith. Ponder these facts—and you will agree that a lying Buddhist is a disgrace to such a transparently honest religion. Likewise backbiting and abusive speech are alien to the pure spirit of Buddhism. One day a foolish man abused the Buddha. The Buddha waited until he had finished and then asked: "Son, if a man declined to accept a present made to him, to whom would it belong?" The abuser replied: "In that case it would belong to the man who offered it." Then the Buddha continued, "My son, you have railed at me, but I refuse to accept your abuse and request you to keep it to yourself. Will it not be a source of misery to you? As the echo belongs to the sound, and the shadow to the substance, so misery will overtake the evil-doer without fail." Of the backbiter or slanderer, the Buddha said, "The slanderer resembles one who flings dust at another when the wind is contrary. The dust simply returns to him who threw it." And "What the backbiter gathers there he spreads abroad to cause disruption here. Thus he is a breaker-up of fellowships, no reconciler of those in strife, finds pleasure and delight in quarrels and utters words that incite quarrels." The Buddha was equally critical of the "idle babbler, speaking out of season about non-existent and irrelevant things." No serenity and self-control can be won by the person who constantly excites his mind with idle gossip.

RIGHT CONDUCT

The Sign Number Four on the Noble Eightfold Path calls for conduct that is peaceful, honest, and pure. It recommends observance of the Five Precepts to which Buddhist laymen as well as monks give their loyalty. These precepts will be detailed later. For the present, Right Conduct might be summed up as a mode of existence that does not bring suffering to others or shame on oneself.

RIGHT LIVELIHOOD

This means the avoidance of work that causes suffering to others or makes a decent, virtuous life impossible. And in this modern world Right Livelihood can be one of the most difficult rules to obey. So many kinds of work are harmful to society and are unworthy of a true Buddhist. There are the arms and nuclear warfare industries, the drink trade, occupations involving the slaughter or vivisection of animals, corruptive yellow journalism, dishonest advertising and publicity, and business that includes usury. Buddhism is not a narrow-minded religion. It regards human frailties with understanding and sympathy. Yet the sincere Buddhist cannot profess one code of morality and earn his livelihood in an occupation with another, debased code.

RIGHT EFFORT

This means a course of strenuous self-improvement. It involves the suppression of evil states of mind and, simultaneously, the strenuous development of good states of mind. Right Effort has this fourfold classification:

The effort to avoid evil not yet existing.
The effort to conquer evil which already exists.
The effort to develop good not yet existing.
The effort to preserve the good already developed.

Contrary to widespread belief in the West, Buddhism is no do-nothing religion. True Buddhism abounds in effort and energy. Enthusiastic effort was, indeed, a vital part of the Buddha's teaching. Here are three texts from that great Buddhist manual, the *Dhammapada:* "He who does not rouse himself when it is time to rise, who, though young and strong, is full of sloth, whose will and thoughts are weak, that lazy and idle man will never find the way to enlightenment." "If anything is to be done, let a man do it, let him attack it vigorously!" "By energy, earnestness, discipline, and sense-control, let the wise man build an island for himself that no flood can wash away."

RIGHT MINDFULNESS

The pilgrim on the Path must keep his mind alert. There must be constant vigilance in thought, speech, and action. Conduct and character depend upon the mind behind them. The Buddha was a keen enthusiast for mental alertness. He despised lazy, slothful minds. He urged his followers to be mentally awake in all their actions, in working, eating, drinking, talking, and even in being silent. This awareness, this consciousness of all one's actions and words is one of the great secrets of self-mastery. The sharp, wide-awake, analytical mind is unlikely to lead its possessor into rash and thoughtless speech or conduct. How many disastrous blunders have been made by minds that were only half awake? A man's mind should be an independent observer watching objectively over his body and what goes on around it. Weileng, a pioneer Chinese Buddhist, said, "Our mind should stand aloof from circumstances, and on no account should we allow them to influence the function of our mind." The development of Right Mindfulness is a slow, arduous task. In its early stages we must slow up our thinking processes in order to intensify our awareness of our actions, and of the people and scenes around us. But with practice sharp awareness becomes automatic, and then we are able to form correct judgments and make correct decisions quickly. Success means mastery over much of our fate.

RIGHT CONCENTRATION

The Buddhist does not pray. Instead he concentrates his mind in meditation and thereby reaches a comprehension of Reality. Meditation, as practised in Asia for thousands of years, is comparatively new to the West. Formerly it was regarded here as a useless pagan practice. Today methods of Buddhist and Hindu meditation are studied by many Western psychologists. Those of the school of the late Carl Jung, in particular, believe it has strong therapeutic value. The concentration of all the mental faculties in meditation produces what is called "one-pointedness of mind." In Right Concentration the pilgrim devotes his mind with intensity exclusively to a single object, thought, or problem. Gradually his mental reaction to all outside stimulus disappears and he reaches a state of supreme serenity that can lead on into ecstasy and rapture. In such a state the mind attains transparent clarity during which the truths, such as the nature of sorrow, are at last lucidly comprehended. Finally, in the concentration of a much practiced and fully dedicated Buddhist, reason, emotions, and feelings are lost in Nibbana, the highest state of enlightenment. Later in this book we shall study the stages of meditation as described by the Buddha. The Buddhist layman and particularly the Buddhist novice must not allow himself to be scared away by a meditative procedure that seems so esoteric. Buddhism has no secrets and no magic. Its practices are rational and without obscurity. However the layman and novice can quickly find benefit in simple meditation, which needs no sessions with a teacher or manuals of elaborate instruction. All he has to do is to sit still and concentrate his attention on one article, real or imaginary; or concentrate his thoughts on a single idea or problem. I have met ardent converts to Buddhism in America and Europe who spend hours of their time every week in study on How to Meditate, often with the assistance of an instructor. Yet in Bangkok and Colombo I have met youths and girls, with little education, who without elaborate lessons and complicated formulas, obtain great inspiration from meditation. How do they achieve this? Simply by sitting still in solitude and concentrating. In the outside world these young people carry with them a serenity and compelling charm that are one of the wonderful results of Right Concentration.

So that is the Eightfold Path. And at the end of it the pilgrim who has tried conscientiously to follow the signposts finds himself in what seems to be a new world. Actually it is the same old world with a newly purified person observing it. Now he is calm and self-possessed. Fear has left his heart. People who knew him formerly are astonished by the change and wonder what his secret is.

In my paragraph on Right Conduct I mentioned the recommended observance of the Five Precepts. These five form the foundation of the ethics of the Buddhist laity. When the layman visits the temple on a holy day, or in his private religious exercises, he recites the following:

I take the precept to abstain from killing.
I take the precept to abstain from stealing.
I take the precept to abstain from adultery.
I take the precept to abstain from lying.
I take the precept to abstain from liquor that causes intoxication and heedlessness.

These Precepts are not a table of commandments. Buddhism has no commandments. The acceptance of the Precepts and their ceremonial recitation are voluntary.

"Thou shalt not kill" is one of the Ten Commandments of Christianity. But the prohibition here does not include the wanton slaughter of animals. A Buddhist who hunts animals for sport definitely breaks the First Precept. And no one taking the First Precept could conscientiously watch a bull being tortured in a Spanish ring or a fox being torn to death by hounds at a Virginia hunt. Buddhism is a religion of infinite compassion. Its scriptures abound in kindly references to animals and with parables concerning them. The *Dhammapada* warns that "Whoever strives only for his own happiness, and in doing so hurts or kills living creatures which seek happiness too, he shall find no happiness after death." Elsewhere scriptures and their parables encourage making friends with animals. They suggest that merely to respect animal life is not enough. The world's first animal hospitals were founded by a Buddhist. He was Asoka, the great emperor, who ruled India nearly three hundred years before Christ. We shall discuss his good works in a later chapter. Despite these ideals, the treatment of animals in parts of the Buddhist world is far from perfect. For example, people will respect the lives of dogs, but allow them to wander, hungry and emaciated. The city of Rangoon is overrun with such dogs. None are killed—but at the same time the populace is too poor to feed the wretched animals adequately. However, in Burma wild creatures do not shrink in terror from men as in Europe and America. Buddhism does not condemn killing animals for food, or the destruction of vermin that threaten our safety and health. The Buddha ate meat, and so do many monks today. There is much vegetarianism among Buddhists—but whether or not to eat meat is regarded as a matter for individual conscience. Vegetarians are told that there are worse actions than meat-eating. Says the *Amagandha Sutta,* "Anger, drunkenness, obstinacy, bigotry, deception, envy, self-praise, disparaging others, high-mindedness, evil communications—these constitute uncleanness; not verily the eating of flesh."

The Second Precept—to abstain from stealing—needs no comment. The Third—to abstain from adultery—is interesting when the Buddhist attitude towards sex is considered. It is a realistic attitude. "Of all the lusts and desires," said the Buddha, "there is none so powerful as the sexual urge." But it is recognized as a natural urge and its physical expression is not discouraged in laymen. In the Theravada Buddhist view, marriage is a private, civil affair and unconnected with religion. In parts of the Buddhist world there is still some polygamy, without religious condemnation. And the society of the Buddha's time and country was largely polygamous. Adultery as named in the Precept covers a wider range than unfaithfulness. I heard it explained to a group of young Ceylonese as "Any sexual act that would hurt others in their person or their feelings." In other words, any sexual act likely to increase human suffering. Buddhism, remember, is a religion dedicated to the alleviation of human suffering. Thus adultery is not only to be unfaithful to one's legal spouse. Any sexual conduct that is likely to cause grief to a man's parents or other relatives is also adultery. Of course Buddhism urges its laity to exercise self-control in sex. However, it sees no virtue in the person who, though physically chaste, is unchaste in thought and conversation. Thus the sex-ridden films and books from the United States are often deplored in Buddhist countries as contributing towards the moral corruption of their youth. These give young people unsavory thoughts that in turn result in conversation that disgusts the older generation of Asians. Whereas Western moralists still describe sexual immorality as "bestial," the realistic Buddhists are hinting that this is a slander on the beasts. In a widely-read pamphlet on the Five Precepts, Bhikkhu Silacara of Ceylon writes, "Consider the 'lower animals' as we are pleased to call them, and their sexual behavior. Which really is lower here, the animal or the man? Which acts in a normal, regular manner as regards sexual behavior? And which runs off into all manner of irregularities and perversities? Here it is the animal that is the higher creature and man that is the lower. And why is this? It is simply because man who possesses the mental capacity which, rightly used, could make him master over his sex impulsions, has actually used his mental powers in such deplorable fashion as actually to make himself more slave to those impulsions than are the animals." Lastly, here is a suggestion from Buddhist Scripture on making easier observance of the Third Precept: "If you speak to a woman, do so in purity of heart. Is she old? Regard her as your mother. Is she young? Look upon her as your sister. Is she very young? Then see her as your child."

The Fourth Precept—not to tell untruths—emphasizes the importance the Buddha placed on Right Speech. The Fifth Precept—to abstain from intoxicants—is an important Precept, although it is belittled from time to time by Buddhist commentators. True it is not among the Precepts listed in some scriptural records. But as Buddhism is a religion of mental development and control, surely its followers should never cloud the clarity of their minds either with alcohol or drugs. The Buddha called upon his followers to be at all times mindful, self-possessed and serene. This is exactly what a drunken man is not! Indeed, in conversation with a young layman named Sigala, the Buddha listed "Six disadvantages of indulging in intoxicants—loss of wealth, increase of quarrelling, proneness to illness, loss of reputation, immodest acts, and weakening of brain power." Now Buddhism is not a religion of cranks, and few of its leaders condemn the layman who takes an occasional social drink. In full, the Fifth Precept reads, "I take the Precept to abstain from liquor that causes intoxication and heedlessness." Thus there is nothing evil if the drink is consumed in such a small quantity that the mind remains clear and responsible.

It is important to remember, while discussing Buddhist morality, that its idea of sin differs somewhat from the Christian idea. Sin to the Buddhist is mere ignorance or stupidity. The wicked man is an ignorant man. He doesn't need punishment and condemnation so much as he needs instruction. He is not regarded as "violating God's Commands" or as one who must beg for divine mercy and forgiveness. Rather is it necessary for the sinner's friends to make him reason in the human way and realize that only he can save himself. Buddhism offers man a code, as expressed in the Eightfold Path, the Five Precepts and other formulas. It is up to him to accept or reject it. But study of this simple code and an experimental practice of it will (say the Buddhists) have more chance of reforming a man than will many prayers and rites of penance. For the code is founded on personal experience and upon facts that may be verified. In the words of the Buddha, "When you know for yourselves—these things are moral, these things are blameless; these things are praised by the wise; these things when performed and undertaken, result in well-being and happiness —then do you live and act accordingly." Again it should be stressed that evil acts inevitably produce evil results to the doer, if not in this life then in another. No one can sin without paying the penalty; for pain comes out of evil and happiness comes out of good. The Buddhist does not believe the sinner can escape the consequences in prayerful attempts to bargain with God. If a man thrusts his hand into a furnace he will burn it, and all the prayer in the world won't remove the scars. It is the same with the man who walks into the fires of evil action.

We shall return to more moral teachings of Buddhism later. Meanwhile let us examine the devotional side of the religion. Theravada Buddhism has often been called cold and forbidding. It won't recognize a personal God. It refuses to believe that communion with God can be made through prayer or ritual, or that God can be appeased with sacrifices and offerings. In fact rites and ceremonies are not only described as useless; they are condemned as wrong. Buddhism preaches that the ruthless law of cause and effect is always unalterable. A man's salvation, it repeats, depends upon himself alone. Yet studies of primitive as well as of modern civilizations show how man has always needed a power he can venerate and in which he can find strength. When this hasn't been a god or gods it has been a person or a political institution. Every man wants consolation and inspiration in his loneliness. The intellect and emotions of the Buddhist are sustained by his affectionate veneration for what are called The Triple Gem or Threefold Refuge. These consist of the Buddha, his Teaching and the Community of Monks. The only formality in becoming a Buddhist is, indeed, to repeat the beloved words, quoted in my last chapter:

I take my refuge in the Buddha,
I take my refuge in the Dhamma (Teaching),
I take my refuge in the Sangha (Order of Monks).

Most practicing Buddhists solemnly repeat this formula daily, together with the Precepts. Their faith, their love, their gratitude and joy are with deep emotion focused on this, the Triple Gem of their religion, their Threefold Refuge in the storms of life. The image of the Buddha is displayed in the temples like the Cross on the altars of Christian churches. And devotees will burn incense or lay flowers before it. In Kandy, Ceylon, I heard children—kneeling before such an image—recite:

No other Refuge do I seek.
Buddha is my matchless Refuge.
By might of Truth in these my words,
May joyous victory be mine.

Such scenes, witnessed by non-Buddhists, lead to charges that these Asians "worship idols," and they bring to mind a hymn containing the smug words:

The heathen in his blindness
Bows down to wood and stone!

Of Theravada Buddhism nothing could be more untrue. The Buddha image (known as a Rupa) is the symbol of his life and teaching. It is venerated as representing the man who, in his reflections and subsequent enlightenment, learned transcendental truths that can save mankind from its sorrows. The image is also a symbol and memorial of the Buddha's perfect life and infinite compassion. Thus followers pay homage to the ideals and ideas the image represents. They do not pray to it as to an omnipotent god who must be appeased and flattered with humble entreaties. They do not ask favors of the Buddha image. And as they kneel and meditate they feel close to the Buddha, just as a bereaved husband might feel as he gazes at a photograph of the wife he loved and whose memory he now adores. The life of the Buddha has, throughout the centuries, inspired matchless art. There are many Buddha images of a calm unearthly beauty that move and inspire. In his *Travel Diary of a Philosopher* Count Keyserling wrote, "I know nothing more grand in this world than the figure of the Buddha; it is an absolutely perfect embodiment of spirituality in the visible domain."

"Do not think 'Our teacher is no longer with us,'" said the Buddha before his passing. "The truths and rules of the Order that I have presented and laid down for you, let them be your teacher after I am gone." So the Teaching (or Dhamma, meaning "What is firm and established") is the second precious gem of the religion. We have already looked at the basic portion of this doctrine in the Four Noble Truths and the Eightfold Path. The expanded teachings, in the sermons and dissertations of the Buddha, possess a charm and vitality that seem to bring him to life. They have snatches of delicious humor. There is no hint of such earthy facetiousness in the sayings of Jesus or Mohammed. The Buddha had an answer to almost every question—and often the answer, while uncannily correct, was at the same time laugh-provoking. Perhaps that is why there are no killjoys among lay Buddhists. It would certainly be a reason for the informality of Buddhist temples, with visitors laughing aloud and children even playing games. Buddhism has no equivalent of Sabbath observance laws. The consciences of laymen —without outside pressures—decide what they shall do on holy days. Many men and women, respected by their neighbors as good Buddhists, never go inside a temple. Practical observance of the Teaching is regarded as far more important than prostration in temples of brick and stone. And the Teaching is beloved by people of every range of intellect. Paradoxically, it has a simplicity that seems clear to ordinary folk, while intellectuals, probing deeper, find it rich in subtlety. "My teaching is pure and makes no distinction between noble and ignoble, rich and poor," said its creator. "My teaching is like water which cleanses all without distinction. My teaching is like fire which consumes all things between heaven and earth, great and small. My teaching is like the heavens; for there is ample room in it for all; for men and women, boys and girls, the powerful and the lowly."

Buddhism would not be the practical religion it is without the Third Gem—the Order of Monks, better known as the Sangha or the Order of His Noble Disciples. "Had the Buddha merely taught philosophy," wrote Professor T. W. Rhys Davids, "he might have had as small a following as

Comte." The Order grew into a mighty organization from the five ascetics who were converted by the Buddha's first sermon in the deer park at Sarnath. His teachings were not written down for many years. They were memorized by the faithful members of the Order and passed on, from generation to generation. It was the Order which, through the centuries, gave the masses by example and lesson the significance of the Buddha's gospel. These dedicated men were never priests. They claimed no intercessory or supernatural powers. But they were living illustrations to the world of what Buddhism meant in its highest development. Buddhism might have meant even less than Comte's Positivism to ordinary people today had not the Buddha 2,500 years ago formed this Order to guard and sustain the jewel of the Teaching. These penniless men, with their yellow robes and begging bowls, renounced the world and yet conquered a big portion of it for the fair and noble philosophy of their leader.

3 FETTERS AND REBIRTH

There is widespread agreement that a man is happier when he forgets himself. You will recall many occasions yourself where the cure suggested for a miserable person has been, "He wants taking out of himself." So many activities are based on the desire of people to escape from their solitary thoughts. Sports, the theater, music, parties—what are they but modes of flight from the boresome ego? Drink and drugs are also methods of ego-escapism. At the same time, society regards the dignity and preservation of self or soul as of inherent importance. On the one hand we are told how important self is; on the other we are advised to forget it. This confusion only adds to our miserable self-consciousness. The idea that the little self may not be eternal is to many of us outrageous. Some spend every seventh day observing the belief that the puny self will survive death and go on and on. As the German Buddhist Paul Dahlke wrote, "Like the cackling hen that seeks some place of safety for the egg she wishes to lay, so do we men roam anxiously around, seeking some place in which we can deposit for eternity this precious 'I' of ours." The Buddha's teaching on the vexed problem of self is sensational and unique; it makes Buddhism essentially different from all other religions. The teaching is that there is no such thing as a permanent self or soul! In short, all self-worship is folly and delusion. There are no permanent things at all. Our minds are simply part of this constant change and movement, with no "soul" independent of these. This doctrine is contained in what Buddhism calls the Three Signs of Being. The Signs are:

1. Impermanence
2. Suffering
3. Non-self

We have already discussed Suffering, so we will concentrate upon Impermanence and the resultant doctrine of Non-self. The Buddha taught that all compound things, from men to mountains, are ruled by the law of change. Living things, objects, and institutions may seem lasting to our eyes, but all are changing and all must ultimately meet with dissolution. There is birth or origination, growth, decay, and then death. Nothing survives time. Flux rules the universe and eventually this little world on which we live must dissolve. As Shelley wrote,

Worlds on worlds are rolling ever from creation to decay,
Like the bubbles on a river, sparkling, bursting, borne away.

Nothing *is*. Everything is *becoming*. There is no present —only change. And in these ideas the genius of the Buddha saw what many famous philosophers and scientists were later to teach. Heraclitus, the Greek philosopher, taught that all phenomena were in constant flux, always tending to assume new forms. In what is classed as modern philosophy,

Descartes said all existence is of a passing nature; Hume denied the unities of soul and substance and saw consciousness as a series of fleeting mental states; and Hegel wrote that "the entire phenomenon is a becoming." Schopenhauer, despite his denials, probably got many ideas for his *World as Will and Idea* from the teachings of Buddhism. He kept an image of the Buddha on his writing desk. William James saw consciousness as a stream. "The soul theory is a complete superfluity," he wrote, "so far as accounting for the actually verified facts of conscious experience goes." Bergson called the conscious state "a change without ceasing." It seems extraordinary that the teacher who had come from the princely palace near Kapilavatthu made his pupils familiar with such ideas twenty-five centuries ago—before any of the "modern" philosophers was born.

Why is Suffering one of the trinity of the Signs of Being? Suffering must always be where there is the decay and dissolution of Impermanence. Suffering must also be borne by the individual who persists in thinking that he is a separate entity, apart from the rest of existence, and who refuses to believe that all—including himself—are transitory phenomena. The trouble is that every individual tends to regard himself as the center of the universe and as the one person whose desires must be satisfied. Then, no sooner does he feel that one desire is satisfied, another arises. He also wants to feel a sense of permanence. He even talks of settling down here or there "for good." The failure of being able to do anything "for good" is part of his tragedy. Alas, the man's self *itself* has no individual permanence. His so-called existence is no more than a process of phenomena. Buddhism divides these phenomena into five aggregates (or khandhas). But none of these separately nor all of them together constitutes an ego-entity; therefore, as far as khandhas are concerned, this is non-existent. These five aggregates are material qualities, feeling, perception, co-ordination (habitual tendencies), and consciousness. Of course they are constantly changing, grouping and regrouping. Thus the "ego" or "self" or "soul" has no real existence. The "I" that so many unhappy persons regard as so important is but a constantly changing combination of physical and mental phenomena. However, the Buddhist does not weep over this. He rejoices. Heed the following from the Buddhist scriptures:

Ye that are slaves of the "I," that toil in the service of self from morn to night, that live in constant fear of birth, old age, sickness, and death, receive the good tidings that your cruel master exists not. Self is an error, an illusion, a dream. Open your eyes and awake. See things as they are and you will be comforted. He who is awake will no longer be afraid of nightmares. He who has recognized the nature of the rope that seemed to be a serpent ceases to tremble. He who has found there is no "I" will let go all the lusts and desires of egotism.

And elsewhere the scriptures say:

The foolish man conceives the idea of "self," the wise man sees there is no ground on which to build the idea of "self"; thus he has a right conception of the world and will conclude that all compounds amassed by sorrow will be dissolved again, but the truth will remain.

Then Paul Dahlke, in his classic *Buddhist Essays,* wrote:

The man of knowledge sees through this phenomenal form, the body, and perceives no "I." Where, however, there is no "I," there naturally can be no egoism either, no "I"-mania. In the Buddha's system not only is pessimism done away with, but also the very possibility of pessimism, and of optimism as well. There remains only that unmoved serenity, that conscious indifference, which has its basis in a comprehension to which all things are of equal value.

Acceptance of the truth of the impermanence of self and the world will therefore free a man from much suffering—if he will only make the effort. First, he must end the inordinate slavery to his little ego. He must curb its desires for thousands of satisfactions through his bodily lusts. The aggregates making up his person will always be demanding things, but he must meet such demands with self-control and self-restraint. Second, he must reduce his reliance upon and affection for mere objects and their possession. Daily he must remind himself that they don't matter, because nothing is permanent. Third, he must cease to hate others and end all pride in himself. People are not worth hating; the ego is not worth loving. Human dignity, about which modern statesmen make such smug, pompous speeches, is nonsense. Humility would make more sense, and certainly be nicer. In short, when man ceases clinging to greed, hatred, possessions, and the idea of his own dignity he will be happy. Attachment to these things is like being kept on a chain.

There is no soul, nothing is permanent—but there is the law of cause and effect, or Kamma, the cause of rebirth. Buddhists do not believe in "reincarnation" or the transmigration of souls. However, they do believe in the continual operation of Kamma, the energy produced by a man's deeds of mind, speech, or body. And this Kamma connects his life with the next. Rebirth has been called an extravagant belief. But is it more extravagant than the Christian belief that every baby born is automatically endowed with a soul that will exist forever? Many great minds have believed in rebirth, including Plato, Blake, Goethe, Kant, Swedenborg, and Browning. But let us leave the fascinating subject of Kamma for the present to take up the examination of mankind's ten fetters.

The Buddha saw man as shackled by the chains of his own weaknesses. If some could be broken, man would be happier. Destruction of all the fetters would deliver him from the wheel of rebirths; and the end of the road leading to the blissful state of Nibbana would have been reached.

The Ten Fetters are:

1. Delusion of self
2. Doubt
3. Belief in the efficacy of ceremonies and ritual
4. Sensuality
5. Ill-will
6. Passion for earthly life
7. Desire for future life
8. Pride
9. Self-righteousness
10. Ignorance

Fetter Number One has already been discussed. The second Fetter shackles the man who cannot make up his mind. He is attracted by the Buddha's Teaching. He sees its logicality. Yet when he tries to practise the Teaching he is beset by doubts that he will succeed, and whether it is really true and effective. Since Buddhism expects a man to accept nothing on faith, the doubter deserves, not condemnation, but understanding and patience from others. How can he best solve his doubts? By further study and thought; by consultation with members of the Order or other Buddhist experts. As for the third Fetter, we have already stressed that ceremonies and ritual will achieve nothing in the endeavors of men for self-reform and enlightenment. "Rituals have no efficacy," say the scriptures. "Prayers are vain repetitions, and incantations have no saving power. But to abandon covetousness and lust, to become free from evil passions, and to give up all hatred and ill-will, that is the right sacrifice and the true worship." Fetters Numbers Four and Five—sensuality and ill-will—muddy a mind that in a Buddhist should be as clear and free as a mountain spring. No mind can have clear insight when its owner is full of lusts and ill-will. No one can be self-possessed when he is gripped by these two fetters. The great teachers of Buddhism constantly exhorted man to be mindful, energetic, earnest, serene—which are all impossible to him who lusts and hates. "Cleanse your heart of malice," says the gospel of Buddhism. "Cast out all anger, spite and ill-will. Cherish no hatred, not even against your slanderer, nor against those who do you harm, but embrace all living things with kindness and benevolence."

Do not become too attached to life here on earth, and do not long to live after death. For these two passions—Fetters Six and Seven—do indeed hinder the man who wants to be free. Love of life on earth stimulates the unnatural, morbid fear of death. It creates the hypochondriac, the man who will never take risks, even for the right. He lives in terror that some illness or accident will snuff out his insignificant little life here. Realization that death is inevitable, an irrational terror of the inevitable, shock the Earth-lover into passionate hope for the survival of his soul in a heaven. No man can be happy in such a tempest of fear and hope. It is hard to despise and ignore these manifestations of the instinct for self-preservation. There is, however, a sure method of overcoming it. This is to forget the self in service for other people; it is to turn one's love from inwards to outwards. Become engrossed in helping others and you will forget your own morbid, selfish attachments and hopes. Pride and self-righteousness, the Eighth and Ninth Fetters, are, of course, the antithesis of Buddhism. The Buddha himself started his ministry by killing all his princely pride in acts of self-humiliation. He attained sainthood during his life, but never lost his naturalness, never assumed superior airs. His dissertations and parables were never pompous. He had time for the most humble of men and women. He never lost his human sense of fun. Buddhists disapprove of those who boast of their religious experiences. It is the worst form for one to claim that in his meditation he has attained more mystical insight than have his brothers. I have been much impressed by the simplicity of Buddhists—both monks and laymen—who in various ways have attained distinction. Who, for example, could be less proud and self-righteous than U Nu, of Burma? I have seen him as Prime Minister, listening long to fierce, ill-founded criticism thrown at him by young journalists at Rangoon press conferences, and then humbly apologizing to them for his shortcomings. Ignorance —Tenth and last Fetter—is often called the Root of All Evil. But the meaning of ignorance in this case should be made clear. It does not mean being unlettered or lacking in rudimentary knowledge. It means simply lack of knowledge of the Four Noble Truths, the Eightfold Path, and other teachings of the Buddha. The argument is that once these are reasoned about and put to the test, they will be found to be true in reality and not merely in name. All men are born into ignorance—and that is the reason for the tragedy of existence. They do not know that giving way to their instinctive cravings is the cause of all the sorrow and suffering. They do not know that to control these and to follow a few simple rules of conduct will give them the equanimity and serenity that is true happiness. Fortunately, the ignorance of a small proportion of the billions of humanity has been banished by comprehension of the Buddha's message. The Buddha referred to those who were ignorant, in that they had not heard and comprehended the Teaching, as "worldlings." And he said, "All worldlings are insane." That outlook on an erring, muddlesome mankind is saner and kinder than blind condemnation. Mankind is not consciously wicked; it simply does not understand. "The world is full of sin and sorrow," says a passage in the Buddhist Scriptures, "because it is full of error. Men go astray because they think that delusion is better than truth. Rather than truth they follow error, which is pleasant to look at in the beginning but causes anxiety, tribulation and misery. The Teaching is the truth. The Teaching is the sacred law. The Teaching alone can deliver us from error, sin, and sorrow."

There are lovely passages telling how, when the first five Fetters are broken by a man, he moves into a state of purity, and how, with the breaking of the other five, he overcomes all sorrow. "To him who has finished the Path and gone beyond sorrow, who has freed himself on all sides and cast away every fetter, fever and grief are no more. . . . He whose senses have become tranquil, like a horse well broken-in; who is free from pride, of the lust of the flesh and the lust of ignorance—even the gods envy him. Such a person, whose conduct is right, is as undisturbed as the broad earth; as unmoved as a pillar at the city gate; as unruffled as a pellucid lake."

Buddhism loves to enumerate and to list. Many of its followers pay special attention to what are called The Five Hindrances. These are:

1. Sensuality or Greed
2. Ill-will
3. Sloth and Torpor
4. Worry and Flurry
5. Doubt

Three of these Hindrances are, of course, also among the Ten Fetters. The remaining ones—Sloth and Torpor, and Worry and Flurry—seem to be outstanding impediments to contentment and mental health in this present age. Indeed, when I listed the Five Hindrances to the chief of a large publishing corporation he said he would experimentally reflect upon them every morning. A month later he expressed amazement at the stimulus that "meditation" on the Five Hindrances had brought to his mind and efficiency. "By conscientiously trying to evade those Hindrances," he added, "I have become more alert and, even in times of greatest stress, worry and flurry have been replaced by calmness and self-control. Then, by crushing thoughts of ill-will, my relations with my staffs have become much happier."

Now for the details of Kamma. Adherence to the Eightfold Path and the Five Precepts, and the snapping of the Ten Fetters, are so important because of the relentless law of cause and effect that rules the universe. Every action produces an effect. And, of course, the effect of an evil action will be evil. Buddhists believe in the operation of this law in the moral as well as the physical sphere. They agree with the Christian text that "Whatsoever a man soweth, that shall he also reap." In short, the man who inflicts suffering on others will sooner or later have to suffer himself. Human actions (according to Buddhism) form the energy of Kamma. Sometimes we have seen this law of moral causation bring retribution to the wrongdoer in his lifetime. Yet it is often noticeable how many of the wicked seem to flourish. There are few of us who do not know men and women who, despite the misery their cruelty, trickery, or greed have brought upon others, nevertheless appear to live on in happiness and prosperity. What, in such cases, has happened to the law of causation? Actually it has been active. Actions of the wrongdoers have created bad Kamma that will be manifested in later lives if not in the present lives. The bill for the evil actions will eventually be paid—with suffering. Now this is how Kamma works. A man lives a life of good and evil actions, and then comes inevitable death. But his volitional deeds have created the energy of Kamma that does not die with his body. It moves into another being just being born. Under the force of Kamma the elements of form, sense, consciousness, and mental energy which were in the man who died are reconstituted in the new life. This new person has not the "soul" of the last (Buddhists do not believe in souls), but he does have the latter's characteristics and he does inherit the old moral debts. These debts must be repaid in the new life or in lives that come after it. Thus sometimes we meet people, of apparently blameless character, whose lives are filled with disaster and suffering. "What have they done to deserve such tragedy?" we ask. The Buddhist would sympathize—but at the same time he would believe that the tragedies were due to wrongdoing in a previous life or lives. Have these sufferers memory of any previous life and its misdeeds? In most cases such remembrance seems unlikely; so the retribution seems unjust. But I have stressed that Buddhists do not believe in a benevolent deity or in a world where kindness is the natural law. Kamma works mechanistically; but never is there a *deus ex machina*. The Buddhist records, without hint of mitigation, teach:

According to the seed that's sown,
So is the fruit ye reap therefrom.
Doer of good will gather good,
Doer of evil, evil reaps.
Sown is the seed, and thou shalt taste
The fruit thereof.

Every man is architect of his own fortunes. Much of what we enjoy or endure today is due to our actions, if not in the present lives, then in previous lives, through the Kammic force. This force or energy has been compared to an electric current. The light bulb wears out, like the body, but the current still flows and will illumine a new bulb (body) that will take the place of the old. Or Kammic energy may be likened to a flame from one lamp wick. From this flame another lamp is lighted. Thus does Kamma move from one body to another. The movement from life to life goes on and on through a succession of births and deaths until the current or energy of bad Kamma is consumed and no more is being generated. This happens when the individual has conquered craving and attachment, when purity at last brings him to the rest and peace of Nibbana, with no more rebirth, woe, despair, and suffering. We shall be discussing Nibbana later. These ideas of the Buddha on rebirth are often compared with those of Plato. But Plato saw rebirth not as mere Kamma but as the transmigration of an immortal soul. Plato, like the Buddha, believed in an implacable law of moral justice. He was bitter at the idea that sacrifices could bribe the gods to save a man from the consequences of his evil deeds, and he said that the soul got what it deserved. Plato suggested we acquired from previous existences the knowledge which we are inclined to regard as innate. But the Buddha believed we inherited far more than that. A young man asked him, "Why is it that we find amongst mankind the shortlived and the longlived, the healthy and diseased, the ugly and the beautiful, those of little importance and the powerful, the poor and the rich, the low-born and high-born, the ignorant and the wise?" The Buddha replied, "All living beings have Kamma as their own, their inheritance, their congenital cause, their kinsman, their refuge. It is Kamma that differentiates beings into low and high states." Elsewhere the scriptures say that, "Depending on the difference in Kamma appears the difference in the birth of beings, high and low, base and exalted, happy and miserable. Depending on the difference in Kamma appears the difference in individual features of beings, as beautiful and ugly, high-born or low-born or deformed. Depending on the difference in Kamma appears the difference in worldly conditions of beings as gain and loss, fame and disgrace, blame and praise, happiness and misery."

Now, it should be made clear, Buddhists do not believe that all things happening to persons are due to past Kamma. We have a big measure of free will which makes us responsible for our actions. Circumstances affect Kamma but we need not be driven into wicked acts against our volition. Here then is a religion of noble self-reliance. The Buddha named many other conditions, in addition to Kamma, affecting human fate. We inherit some of the characteristics of our parents; we are influenced by environment and chemico-physical causes. Scientist Julian Huxley, in his work *The Stream of Life,* writes of "some genes that control color, others height or weight, others fertility or length of life, others vigor and the reverse, others shape and proportions." Huxley adds that "for mental characters, especially the more complex and subtle ones, the proof is more difficult, but there is every evidence that they are inheritable, and no evidence that their inheritance is due to a different mechanism from that for bodily characters." It is here that Buddhism disagrees with contemporary biology. "The theory of heredity," writes G. P. Malalasekera, of the World Fellowship of Buddhists, "cannot satisfactorily account for the birth of a criminal in a long line of honorable ancestors, for the birth of a saint in a family of evil repute, for the arising of infant prodigies, men of genius, and great spiritual teachers." So Buddhists ask the biologists how William Sidis, American child genius, was able to read and write at two and master six languages at eight; how John Stuart Mill read Greek at three and how Mozart wrote a sonata at four.

Acceptance of the theory of Kamma and rebirth will settle many problems regarding life which previously seemed insoluble. It brings a reasonable explanation to circumstances and events, to the tragedies and comedies of life that otherwise would make the world seem one vast madhouse or the plaything of a crazed deity. Belief in Kamma and rebirth results in a lasting sense of calm and understanding. Life ceases to anger and surprise us; death loses its terrors. No longer do we despairingly utter those useless words, "Why does God let such things happen?" When misfortunes strike us, we realize that payment is being made for wrong actions in a previous life. The debts are being wiped out. And we know that by observance of the Eightfold Path and the

Precepts we can create good Kamma that will bring us happiness and peace. When others mistreat us we can accept their conduct with serenity and without a tinge of anger or hatred; for well do we know that one day, without a shadow of doubt, they will have to pay for their misdeeds. We never condemn evildoers as hopeless cases. For they have the power to reform themselves. They are never beyond the redemption of good Kamma. The inequality of mankind, the wide differences of character between parents and their children, the birth of genius to mediocre parents, accidents and sudden death—all are understood when Kamma is understood.

Does any of us remember past lives? And can the theory of re-birth explain the weird feeling we sometimes experience, when apparently visiting a new place, that we have been there before—but how and when we cannot rationally explain? Dante Gabriel Rossetti expressed this mysterious feeling in the verse:

I have been here before,
But where or how I cannot tell;
I know the grass beyond the door,
The sweet, keen smell,
The sighing sound; the lights around the shore.
You have been mine before,
How long ago I may not know;
But just when at that swallow's soar
Your neck turned so,
Some veil did fall—I knew it all of yore.

The Buddha said he could recall thousands of his past lives. "When I want to," he told his followers, "I can recollect my various states of birth. For instance, one birth, two, five, ten . . . and a hundred thousand. I can recall the various destructions and renewal of eras. I lived there; I was named thus. I belonged to such a family, of such a caste, was thus supported. I had this and that pleasant and painful experience, had such a length of life, disappeared thence and appeared elsewhere. There too I lived. Thus can I call to mind in all their essential details and characteristics, in many diverse ways, my past states of existence." Throughout its 2,500 years of history thousands of followers of Buddhism have claimed to have recalled minute details of past lives while in the depths of meditation. Today—in this century—it is common for a Buddhist to confide in close friends the marvellous recollections of previous states. Buddhist parents, too, will often claim that their prattling young children name people and describe environments that obviously belong to a previous existence. However, the publicizing of such claims and stories is not encouraged. This is because so many modern Buddhist leaders want their religion to appeal to public reason rather than to the mob's passion for anything approaching the mystical or bizarre. Besides, too much publicity given to recollections of past lives might encourage unscrupulous quacks to pose as Buddhist "mystics." Nevertheless a quiet but thorough inquiry into the alleged memory of past lives of hundreds of Burmese and Ceylonese citizens has been made by Mr. Francis Story, a British Buddhist and Pali scholar. Story has gathered the "Kammic recollections" of adults and children in many towns and villages. He has also investigated the ancestral history and ancestral environments of most of those he has interviewed. "I have met children," Story told me, "who accurately describe great grandparents who died before their birth. These children also talk intimately of the great grandparents' contemporaries, and give details of buildings that ceased to exist centuries ago. I have proved enough to be convinced of the doctrine of Kamma and rebirth." In *The Soul of a People,* first published at the end of the last century, H. Fielding Hall tells of his surprise at meeting in Burma many persons who claimed to remember their past lives. The doctrine of Kamma first seemed to Fielding Hall "a mystery such as I could not understand." He added, "But when I went to the people I found that it was simple enough to them; for I found they remembered their former lives often, that their children, young children, could tell who they were before they died, and remember details of their former existence. As they grew older the remembrance grew fainter and fainter, and at length almost died away. But in many children it was quite fresh, and was believed in beyond possibility of a doubt by all the people."

All such evidence is impressive and exciting. Yet it is still difficult for anyone reared on Christian theology fully to accept the doctrines of Kamma and rebirth. Particularly hard it is to believe in the possibility of the continuity of consciousness between the present life and past lives. But Buddhism doesn't expect us to accept anything on faith. We can study the Teaching conscientiously, leave aside anything that, to our own mind seems impossible and unreasonable, and yet still love the Buddha and observe much of his wonderful message on how life should be lived. There is no such thing as excommunication in Buddhism. It can be your refuge, whatever your doubts. All it asks of you is sincerity. Personally I believe in Kamma. If the law of cause and effect operates totally in the physical sphere, then I believe that its operation is also total in the moral sphere. I believe that my evil actions in this life will create Kamma that will move into lives that follow mine. However, I find it difficult to accept fully the idea that such transplanted Kamma will carry with it any of the consciousness I have in this life. This is an honest difficulty. It would be hypocritical if I did not record it together with the many features of the Buddhist gospel that I wholeheartedly accept.

The aim of the earnest Buddhist is eventually to end his succession of rebirths and to attain Nibbana (or Nirvana). But before discussing Nibbana let us glance at what Buddhism calls the Law of Dependent Origination. The Buddha saw life as a wheel or chain of causation that started with ignorance. He endeavored to explain this through the Law which is repeated no fewer than ninety-six times in the Theravadin Scriptures. Its premise is that all the poor human qualities that attract bad Kamma spring from tragic ignorance. Here is the Law:

> From ignorance come the dispositions which lead to rebirth.
> From the dispositions comes consciousness or cognition.
> From consciousness come name and form (personality).
> From name and form come the five senses and the mind.
> From the five senses and the mind comes contact.
> From contact comes feeling.
> From feeling comes craving.
> From craving comes grasping, or attachment to existence.
> From grasping comes becoming.
> From becoming comes birth.
> From birth come old age, sickness, death.

Now for Nibbana (or Nirvana). This is the state reached by the man who wins perfection on the Eightfold Path, who breaks all Ten Fetters, who conquers the craving, the greed, hatred, and delusion which are the origin of all suffering and sorrow. This conquest of evil means that he creates no more bad Kamma to cause a rebirth. His long series of births and rebirths, of lives of pain, come to an end. The man is said now to enter Nibbana. But what does this mean? If there is no lasting, intrinsic self how can he survive beyond death? Does this man, through the perfection of his virtue, become annihilated? Or does he enjoy the peace of Nibbana during his lifetime and then become snuffed out forever on his death? What precisely does Nibbana mean, anyway? Many books, contradicting one another, have been written in answer to such questions. Explanations in incomprehensible jargon by sincere but muddle-headed Buddhist speakers and writers have only added to the confusion surrounding the word. We might make a fresh start with the concise definition of Nirvana (Nibbana) in the *Oxford Pocket Dictionary*—"Extinction of individuality and absorption into the supreme spirit as the Buddhist highest good." A man attains Nibbana when he overcomes the delusion of self. He feels submerged in an unchangeable, eternal spirit or stream. This is a state that cannot be comprehended by our finite mind with its worldly limitations, but many Buddhists have claimed to have understood it in deep meditation, although they have not been able to put it into words. Those who have totally subdued self by the extinction of all greed, hatred, and delusion, have been rapturously happy in their lifetime and have at the same time looked forward to death with equal happiness. Many of them have believed, not in extinction, but in the submersion of their individual consciousness with a universal, infinite consciousness. I realize there is a vagueness in these explanations that might leave critical minds unsatisfied. But in the words of Professor

F. Harold Smith in his *Buddhist Way of Life,* "Nibbana is then a negative conception in relation to the world of existence, but a positive conception as known in mystic experience." And few of us are privileged to attain such mystic experience.

Then there can be no precise knowledge on Nibbana beyond this life. The Buddha said that "the very gods envy the bliss of him who has escaped from the floods of passion and climbed the shores of Nibbana." However, when the Buddha was asked about the life after death of one who has won Nibbana, he did not reply. He suggested that mere speculation on the question of a future life could not contribute anything to the supreme peace and wisdom that constituted Nibbana. Perhaps he meant that the question of eternal life was beyond the conception of the finite intellect, but that concentration upon the Eightfold Path, rather than upon what may come after death, would give a man supernormal faculties that would enable him to comprehend everything. Literally the word Nibbana means "blown out" or "extinguished like a flame." The most reliable of Buddhist scriptures suggest the sense of Nibbana in religion is the blowing-out or extinguishing of craving. One passage says, "Nibbana, Nibbana, so they say, friend Sariputta—but what, my friend, is Nibbana?" "It's the destruction of greed, the destruction of hate, the destruction of illusion—this, friend, is what is called Nibbana." A great student of Buddhism, Professor Max Müller, challenged the idea that Nibbana meant the extinction of death. "If we look in the *Dhammapada* at every passage where Nibbana is mentioned," he said, "there is not one which would require that its meaning should be annihilation, while most, if not all, would become perfectly unintelligible if we assigned to the word Nibbana that meaning." Another scholar, Professor S. Radhakrishnan, sees Nibbana as the opposite of extinction. He writes, "Through the destruction of all that is individual in us, we enter into communion with the whole universe, and become an integral part of the great purpose. Perfection is then the sense of oneness with all that is, has ever been and can ever be. The horizon of being is extended to the limits of reality."

The man who has broken the Ten Fetters, thereby moving into Nibbana, is known to Buddhists as an Arahat. His is a state of happiness and peace. And it is believed that his freedom from the attachments of the senses and passions give him an insight into Nibbana that is still shrouded from those who have not reached perfection. However, an inordinate desire to solve problems of "survival" is contrary to the whole spirit of Buddhism. The true Buddhist must have no passion for earthly life and no desire for future life. These are two of the Fetters that impede his spiritual progress. Again I say that the Buddhist's life must be bold and brave. For him there is no "pie in the sky."

4 THE MONKS

The marvel of Buddhism is that it has lasted so long. Other ancient philosophies, such as Platonism and Stoicism, have survived only in a state of embalmment in the interests of narrow academic study; or they have been incorporated into other systems of thought. They are museum pieces that engross and inspire without arousing emotional fervor. Yet, after 2,500 years, the flower of Buddhism remains fresh and unfaded in the comeliness of immortal youthfulness. The philosophy fascinates the learned scholar in his university. It also illumines the lives of millions of simple peasants. It is still the faith to live by, with the few doctrines that solve the problems of existence and conduct for masses who have no time or opportunity for higher education. All the more wonderful, Buddhism has never been imposed by force. Again we must recall how organized Christianity has, from time to time, used war and persecution in the interests of its preservation and expansion. Sometimes acceptance of the Christian faith and its observance have been made compulsory, with penalties of death or prison for the disobedient.

For example, the Cross was first planted in South America at the point of the sword. Dreadful lingering death was imposed upon thousands of those "heathen" who failed to surrender to the merciless invaders who carried the Cross. If Jesus of Nazareth could be aware of the sadistic outrages committed throughout the world in His name He would be horrified; for the essence of His teaching was gentleness and love. The tragedy was that those who came after Jesus and consolidated His church, enthusiastically incorporated into it the evil traditions of the Old Testament with its angry, revengeful Deity; its doctrines of fire and brimstone. It is true that barnacles of superstition have often clung to Buddhism in its long voyage through the ages. However, murder, persecution, intolerance, and hate were never part of it. Never in Buddhism has the spirit of loving-kindness been usurped by murder, torture, and bloodthirsty intimidation. These have been Christianity's great tragedy. The Child, once innocent and fair, lived far into adulthood—but evil thoughts and deeds so marred her looks that she became difficult to recognize. Buddhism, on the other hand, is older than Christianity yet her eyes are unclouded by the sadness of regret and her smile is still innocent.

How has this religion and philosophy of peace and nonviolence managed to survive for so long? How has it retained its noble principles in a world where force and coercion dominate? The answer is in the unswerving faithfulness of the Third Gem—the Order of Monks. The Buddha told his first monks to "Go forth as wanderers for the sake of the many, for the welfare of the many, out of compassion for the world, for the good and weal and the gain of gods and men. Teach ye the truth, lovely in its origin, lovely in its progress, lovely in its consummation. In the spirit and in the letter, proclaim the higher life in all its fullness and purity." Ages have passed since those words were spoken. But in each of these ages there were the men in the yellow robes "going forth as wanderers" and "teaching the truth." Of course there were monks who were corrupt, who thought of themselves rather than of the people, who failed to master the Buddha's teaching or did not preach it. Nevertheless there were a sufficient number of faithful monks, from age to age, to preach the doctrines undefiled and to fill millions with its spirit.

Many have attacked Buddhism by criticizing its Order of Monks (Sangha). The existence of so many monks has, indeed, strengthened belief in the fallacy that Buddhism is a religion of escape from reality. The idea is that the man in the yellow robe moons about meditating and praying, while begging his food from a laity he despises. The ignorant compare the Sangha with those Roman Catholic orders whose members wall themselves up in monasteries or with those who exercise priestly functions. But the Buddhist monks meditate without praying. They are not priests, nor have they any status as intermediaries between laymen and God. In fact, the Buddha warned his monks (bhikkhus) never to give themselves airs of superiority over the laity. He said, "There is no distinction between the monk who has taken his vows and the man of the world who lives with his family. There are hermits who fall into perdition, and humble householders who rise to the rank of prophets. . . . An ordained disciple must not boast any superhuman perfection. The disciple who, with evil intent and from covetousness, boasts of superhuman perfection, be it in heavenly visions or miracles, is no longer my disciple. Monks, I forbid you to employ any spells or supplications. These are useless; for the law of Kamma rules all things."

Ancient images and statuary do not depict the Buddha in meditation only. They also represent him in active attitudes of calling the earth to witness, of teaching, and of dauntlessness. The historic records show him clearly as a person of energy and action. He loved his periods of retreat and solitude. Nevertheless at regular seasons he moved from place to place with tremendous physical and mental activity. His mind was wide awake. It sparkled with original and inspiring ideas. He had the gifts of humor, irony, satire. For sheer intellectual charm and grace, the recorded conversations of the Buddha are equalled in literature only by the Socratic Dialogues of Plato.

The example the Buddha gave to his disciples was one of participation in the world and not of escape. They were to abandon craving and desire, but they were also to move about with "friendship and compassion." Monks must avoid a life of pleasure, "for that is degrading and vain." But they must also avoid a life of self-mortification, "for that is useless and vain." When flatteringly complimented for his "simple life and solitude," the Buddha replied, "That can hardly be, for while some of my disciples affect ascetic practices, I some days eat more, or wear laymen's clothes, or accept invitations to dinner, or dwell indoors or among my own followers and those of other sects." The Buddha taught and recommended mental concentration and meditation as means to an end—not as an end in itself. T. W. Rhys Davids in his *Early Buddhism* says that, while ecstatic meditation was admitted as part of the training of the monk, "it was not the highest or the most important part, and might be omitted altogether." "The States of Rapture are called Conditions of Bliss, and are regarded as useful for the help they give towards the removal of mental obstacles to the attainment of Arahatship. Of the thirty-seven constituent parts of the Buddha's teaching they enter into one group of four. To seek for Arahatship in the practice of ecstasy alone is considered a deadly heresy. So these practices are both pleasant in themselves and useful as one of the means to the end proposed. But they are not the end, and the end can be reached without them." What then were and are the true aims of the Order? They are mindfulness, wisdom, zest, energy, joyfulness, serenity, equanimity, love, compassion. These lead towards perfection and enlightenment. Meditation helps too. But in excess, meditation can become harmful self-indulgence. This is a truth that annoys many Western people who "take up" Buddhism as a fad and a recreation rather than as a way of self-improvement and deliverance.

The Buddhist monk, then, seeks to deliver himself from the bonds of desire while at the same time serving as an example to the laity. He claims no superior knowledge or priestly powers. However, he does endeavor to lead the ordinary men and women along the Noble Eightfold Path. Anybody who feels the call may become a monk. There are no life-long vows and the acceptance of no dogma is demanded. The monk is not expected blindly to accept Buddhist teachings, as the Roman Catholic must accept his Church's creed. Every doctrine must be submitted to reason. "O monks," said the Buddha, "don't accept even my own words out of respect for me. You must examine them on the touchstone of your reason, as the goldsmith tests the purity of his gold by putting it on a fire." Dissension in the

Order is an evil thing, and there must always be a spirit of forgiveness and tolerance. Once the Buddha sternly condemned the Order for excommunicating one of its members for his opinions. "Don't imagine," he said, "that you are to order the expulsion of a fellow for this or that, saying 'It occurs to us to expel this monk.' "

The first Buddhist monks were Kondanna and his four companions, converted by the Buddha in the deer park of Sarnath. And in the first chapter I told how swiftly the Order expanded. In those early days it seemed to have a special appeal to aristocrats and intellectuals, notwithstanding the Buddha's contempt for the rigid social grades and distinctions of his time. In the joy at the wonder of his message, kings and princes begged the Buddha to teach more to them and their subjects. For the Sangha—"the community of one caste"—they gave woods, parks, and meadows. To these the monks would retire, not only for contemplation but also to receive and instruct those who wanted to learn. Typical was the Bamboo Grove at Kosala, given by the King of Magadha. Wealthy merchants shared with royalty the desire to help the monks. There was, for example, the merchant Anathapindika, who built a large monastery on Jetavana Park in Kosala. The rule was established that the monks would always spend the rainy season in such centers, while the rest of the year would be spent in pilgrimage, wandering and begging. Imagine the stir caused in caste-conscious ancient India by an Order where pariah and Brahmin were declared equals. Small wonder that, in their perplexity, aristocrats should ask the Buddha how such defiance of what they regarded as a divine law was possible. To one Brahmin who questioned the Buddha about his caste came this moving reply:

I am not a Brahmin or rajah's son
Nor am I a merchant nor any one at all.
I know the lineage of the average folk,
And I fare in the world, a sage, with nothing.
Wearing a monk's robe, homeless, I go;
My head is shaven and I am extinguished as to self,
Without taint of human concerns;
Unmeet it is to ask me of my lineage.

The Buddha identified snobbery with a bondage keeping man from the freedom of mental and spiritual development. He said, "Those infatuated by ideas of birth, lineage, and pride of social position are far from the highest wisdom. One must get rid of all such bondage to attain the perfection of wisdom and conduct."

The Buddha suggested many rules for his Order. These ancient rules are still more or less observed (and are regularly recited too) by thousands of monks. Members of the Order must observe the Five Precepts which form also the foundations of the ethics of the Buddhist layman. And they must also observe these five extra precepts:

Not to eat at forbidden times.
To abstain from dancing, singing, music, and acting.
Not to use garlands, unguents, or ornaments.
Not to sleep on a high or broad bed.
Not to receive gold or silver.

The warnings to members of the Order against sloth are frequent; for the monk must be ardent, earnest, and mentally awake at all times. His mind must be clear, sparkling, and bright.

Sloth, say the scriptures, is a drowsy, yawning outlook caused by excessive eating and by giving way to desires.

Unless sloth is repressed it gives rise to pride, malice, doubt, and the discontent that goes with lack of occupation. The aim of the monk is not repose so much as mental sharpness and ceaseless social service. "This is no doctrine for the sluggard," said the Buddha, "but for the man who puts forth virile efforts." The regulations of the Sangha forbid the monk to take solid food except between sunrise and noon. He leaves his bed before daylight, washes himself, and cleans up his abode. Taking his bowl he goes begging from door to door. On his return the monk eats the only meal of the day. In mindful repose he then seeks fuller realization of truth in meditation or thought. And the five biggest subjects for his meditation exercises are love, pity, joy, impurity, and serenity. I shall discuss these later in a chapter on meditation.

The Buddha perhaps followed an age-old custom in having his monks clad in yellow which, according to tradition, was the color worn by wandering ascetics. Traditionally, too, yellow is the color for immortality. The garments of members in the early years of the Order were sewn together from rags. The clothing consisted of two undergarments and one robe, which left the right shoulder uncovered. The monk's eight requisites consisted of no more than three robes, a girdle, alms bowl, razor, needle, and water strainer. The simplicity of attire had to be matched by simplicity of conduct and manner. The first Buddhist monks were exhorted to be gentle, modest, pure in mind and body. They were warned to shun "the four sins of the tongue—lying, slander, abuse, and idle chatter"; to shun "the three sins of the mind—covetousness, hatred, and error. Don't swear but speak decently and with dignity. Don't waste time with empty words. Either speak for a purpose or keep silent."

Finally, the monks were urged to banish from their hearts all ill-will and hatred, and to greet all living creatures in the spirit of loving kindness. Here, indeed, is the ideal of the Sangha and of all Buddhism.

Buddhism has lay sisters who live as nuns, but they do not play as important a part in their religion as do the nuns in Roman Catholicism. I visited a community of lay sisters in Burma. Their monastic mode of life was similar to that of the monks. They also had shaven heads and eyebrows and looked to me more like boys than women. They did not go out begging but had a kitchen with lay cooks. Their behavior towards male members of the Order was one of great deference. The Buddha's attitude towards women seems strange from the point of view of today. At times he was inclined to regard them with some humor mixed with light cynicism. He showed the same kind of impatience towards his stepmother, Pajapati, as Socrates showed towards his wife, Xanthippe. Nevertheless he could on occasions be charming and understanding towards women, such as when he was dinner guest of the reformed prostitute Ambapali. Yet he could, elsewhere, tell his disciples, "I see no single form so enticing and so desirable, so intoxicating and so distracting, such a hindrance to gaining unsurpassed peace from effort—that is to say, monks, as a woman's form." When Ananda asked the Buddha how he should behave towards women, the advice was, "Don't see them."

"But what if we do see them?"

"Don't speak."

"But what if they speak to us?"

"Just keep wide awake, Ananda."

The Buddha, being no congenital ascetic, knew too well female seductiveness and female power. He had been a prince and, in the custom of his time, the most attractive dancing girls would have been installed in the palace for his entertainment and hours of relaxation. He would have known of the female jealousies and rivalries of such a household. Then his marriage to Yasodhara had been idyllically happy. The most moving descriptions in the story of the Buddha's Great Renunciation are those of his farewell glances at his sleeping wife and at the sleeping palace dancing girls. The Buddha had, in a sexual sense, been a worldly young man. Thus the touch of sophistication and cynicism in his remarks about the opposite sex. The fact that the Buddha had, before his mission, tasted the pleasures of sense added to his appeal to laymen. They recognized him as a brother who knew temptation because he succumbed to it; who overcame the weakness of a normal sensuous nature in frustrating the cravings and achieving Nibbana. Here lies one difference between Christianity and Buddhism: In Christianity God became Man; in Buddhism Man became God.

The Order of Nuns was founded only after a show of resistance by the Buddha. It was the achievement of his aunt and stepmother Pajapati, the strongminded woman who refused to take "No" for an answer. On the death of the Buddha's father, the Rajah Suddhodana, she came to him and asked that women, like men, should be allowed to renounce the world for the Yellow Robe and the discipline it signified. The Buddha refused. Twice more she repeated this appeal; each time the refusal was reiterated. But Aunt Pajapati refused to admit defeat. She went home—but only to slash off her hair and to dress herself in a yellow robe. Other women followed her example. They all went to the door of the Buddha to weep and to implore. They were found in this plight by the Buddha's close friend and disciple, Ananda. Women "making a scene" had a faster effect upon the impressionable Ananda than upon the Buddha. Three times he went to his lord with the women's frantic requests to join the Order; again there came a refusal three times. Finally the desperate Ananda, anxious to end the scene at the Buddha's threshold, asked him outright whether a woman "who has left her house for a homeless life" for the discipline of his teaching was capable of reaching perfection. The Buddha replied that yes, she was capable of this. Then Ananda said, "If so, Pajapati, your aunt, was of great service. She was your nurse and foster-mother, and gave you milk. On your mother's death she fed you from her own breast." Ananda followed this reminder with a new appeal that Pajapati be allowed to join the Order. The Buddha relented at last. He offered "eight strict rules" and added that if Pajapati accepted them, she could be ordained. The rules included the following:

> A nun must first salute a monk and rise in his presence, even if he is newly ordained. A nun shall not spend Retreat in a place where there is no monk. Every fortnight a monk will "give admonition" to a meeting of nuns. A nun must not, under any pretext, rebuke or abuse a monk. Utterances (or official pronouncements) may not be made by nuns to monks, but may be made by monks to nuns.

Pajapati accepted the rules with the pledge that "just as a woman or man, who is young and enjoys adornment, after washing the head receives in both hands a garland of lotus or jasmine flowers, and puts it on her head, even so do I accept these eight strict rules, not to be broken while life shall last." The Order of Nuns was launched, and Yasodhara, wife of the Buddha in his early life as Prince Siddhattha, was among its first members. Unless the Buddha was talking ironically, he regretted giving in to the demands of his stepmother. For he told Ananda that "If women had not been given permission to leave the household life for the homeless state under the Teaching, then pure religion would have lasted long and the Good Law would have stood fast for a thousand years. But now that women have received permission, pure religion will not last long. Now, Ananda, the good Teaching will last only 500 years. Just as houses, where there are many women and few men, are the easy prey of robbers, so in the doctrine and discipline in which a woman goes forth, the religious system will not last long." It seems that leaders of the Order agreed with the Buddha and were annoyed with Ananda for sponsoring female membership. After the Buddha's death, the first Buddhist council chided the unfortunate Ananda for it.

This early conflict over the right of women fully to practice Buddhism was unwise and unfortunate. But we may rejoice that the prediction of a life of only 500 years for the "pure religion" has proved to be wrong. We may well believe that the Buddha made this in jest or raillery. Buddhism, to its glory, knows nothing of the persistent anti-feminism of other Eastern religions. It has never been disgraced by such indecent horrors as the harem of the Moslems, the purdah of Hinduism and the suttee of its widows. The tradition of feminine freedom has been maintained until today, when in Ceylon and Burma women are proud, independent, and influential. The Buddhist woman is an individual, not a thing; whereas, even in enlightened Moslem and Hindu communities, the woman is still regarded as an inferior being who owes any social and civic advancement to male condescension more than to right. Then Buddhism has been kinder to women than organized Christianity has been. Jesus never questioned woman's equality with man. There was no woman among His Twelve Disciples, yet in His friendship with Martha and Mary, in His encounters and talks with women He showed unqualified respect. But soon afterwards Paul was to come to degrade the reputation of women because of his obsession that sex was ugly and wicked. The Christian theologians of the Middle Ages succeeded in undermining woman's stature still more. It was Eve who tempted Adam in the Garden of Eden and brought about his fall. Eve was the original cause of Original Sin. Thus the theologians argued in their blindness. Their passion for feminine virginity made even marriage seem indecent and degrading. Their argument for the innate perfection of Jesus was based largely on the claim that He was "conceived without sin" in the womb of "Mary most pure." All kinds of excuses had to be given for marriage as if its physical union were something improper. Even the Anglican Prayer Book went at lengths to explain that marriage "was ordained for a remedy against sin, and to avoid fornication; that such persons as have not the gift of continency might marry, and keep themselves undefiled members of Christ's body." What is this but an endorsement of Paul's pronouncement that "It is better to marry than to burn"? So through the Christian ages the woman—successor to Eve, the temptress—was "put in her place," which was always second place. Meanwhile, in the countries of pure Buddhism, woman shared equality with the man. In Ceylon, Burma, and Thailand, the wife had no inferior status to the husband. She did not wear a wedding ring or adopt her husband's name. Her property did not become his. She had the last word in the upbringing of children. Married women ran their own businesses, made their own decisions. Rights that these Eastern women had enjoyed for centuries were regarded as revolutionary and daring when introduced into the Christian West in this century after the agitation of such "modernists" as Henrik Ibsen and Bernard Shaw. Shaw called the female who defied sexual inequality and demanded freedom, "The New Woman." But in Asia that woman was many centuries old.

Buddhism among millions of Asian women is no mere form but a living faith. Probably the woman possesses a more sensitive understanding of the Buddha's teaching because, more than the man, she knows the meaning of physical suffering and its universality through her own experience. Both man and woman know the pleasure of procreation; only woman knows the agony of childbirth. The Buddha said that birth was as full of suffering as decay and death. How well the woman knows this! Personal beauty in a man is unimportant; in woman it cannot be underestimated. The pretty girl, the beautiful woman, are made conscious of their loveliness by the admiration of the community. Thus when a woman grows old and her beauty fades, she cannot but recognize and believe the Buddha's teaching on the evanescence of all living things. She sees her reflection in the mirror, surveys the lines and wrinkles of time and knows what the Exalted One meant when he said that all compound things must disintegrate.

Women are important figures in some of the most moving episodes of the Buddha's life. There was his dinner with Ambapali, the reformed prostitute. Then it was through Kisa Gotami, a bereaved young mother, that the Buddha emphasized in a starkly practical manner his doctrine of the universality and omnipresence of suffering. The story of Kisa Gotami and her quest for the mustard seed is one of the great classics of the Buddhist Scriptures. When the baby son of

Kisa Gotami died she was unable to believe it. She carried the little corpse from neighbor to neighbor begging "for medicine to revive him." The neighbors replied that the baby was dead. Kisa Gotami, still numb to reality, was eventually led to the Buddha. "Lord and master," she cried, "give me medicine to cure my boy." The Buddha replied, "Then bring me a handful of mustard seed—but it must come from a home where nobody has lost a husband, parent, or friend." Filled with faith that the child would be saved, Kisa Gotami went from house to house begging for mustard seed. All offered to give her some; but when she asked whether anybody had died in their house, their faces fell. "Alas," some said, "there are a few alive—but the dead are many. Don't stir up our old sorrows." Kisa Gotami knocked on the doors of many houses, but there was none that had not, at some time or other, been visited by death. At last worn out and bereft of hope, the mother sat at evening on the roadside still clutching the cold, lifeless body of her son. Her eyes were attracted by the lights of the city that lay before her below. The lights would flicker, as if being blown out and lit again. And as the evening moved into night, the city sank into sleep and all the lights went out. Thinking about those city lights, now extinguished, Kisa Gotami at last accepted the fact that her baby was dead. In her quest of the mustard seed she had learned that death in all families was inevitable. And looking at the lights she had suddenly associated them with the life of man, flickering for a time, then going out. "My grief is a selfish thing," Kisa Gotami exclaimed to herself. "Death is common to all." The mother had the body buried and resolved to abandon a sorrow that she now recognized as selfishness. She returned to the Buddha and took refuge in the Teaching. Now he told her that "the life of people in this world is short and intermingled with pain. Those who are born must some time die. They are always in danger of death, just as ripe fruits are in danger of falling. In a world afflicted with death and decay wise people do not grieve. For they accept the rules of the world."

Although Pajapati and her friends fought so hard for the establishment of the Order of Nuns, it flourished only for a few centuries and then declined. No one has ever satisfactorily explained why. But while the Order was young and strong it contributed much to the literary and poetic riches of Buddhism. The nuns composed psalms of bewitching beauty rejoicing in the revelation of their religion and in the loveliness of the natural scenes in which they meditated. Brave pioneers, these women looked the sorrow and tragedy of life in the face. But they found joy in the escape from these through the abandonment of desire. The psalms of the nuns were handed down orally for generations until they were finally recorded in writing. Mrs. Rhys Davids, who translated these psalms from the Pali, wrote that "there is at times a combined beauty of word and image entitling them to rank as world poetry."

5 ASOKA, BUDDHIST EMPEROR

The transforming power of Buddhism has swiftly made new personalities of all kinds of men, from kings to peasants, throughout the ages. It has changed individual men and women; it has changed entire nations. The Emperor Asoka of India is probably history's greatest example of this transformation. The Teaching turned him from the mass murder of military conquest to a benevolence that brought peace and happiness to millions. It inspired him to send missionaries to many lands. Asoka thereby made an enormous conquest. He won Ceylon for Buddhism. This was earlier than 200 B.C. And today Ceylon is still predominantly Buddhist. Indeed it is possible that without the dynamic zeal of Asoka, Buddhism might have remained a local religion, confined to one area of India. "So far as we can see," wrote Vincent Smith in his *Asoka, Buddhist Emperor of India,* "the transformation of this local sect into a world religion is the work of Asoka alone. What St. Paul was to Christianity, so, in his way, was Asoka to Buddhism." But Asoka did not distort the teaching of the Buddha as St. Paul distorted the teaching of Jesus. He passed on the Teaching in its original purity.

Asoka was born about 304 B.C. He was a son of King Bindusara and grandson of the great Chandragupta, founder of the Mauryan dynasty. The family had built an empire upon force and cunning, upon cruelty and slavery. The young Asoka was faithful to these traditions, and assiduously schemed and plotted to win supreme power for himself. The sixteen wives of Bindusara had borne more than one hundred sons. Asoka, after the death of his father, saw that his kindred must be destroyed if his lust for power was to be fully satisfied. So, according to some records, Asoka rose against the other sons of his father, killing ninety-nine of them. This was nothing compared with the slaughter and tortures that were to follow when Asoka, intent upon consolidating the empire, waged war upon Kalinga (Bengal). The King of Kalinga had a defense force of 60,000 infantry, 1,000 cavalry, and 700 fighting elephants. The armies of Asoka overwhelmed them and wallowed triumphantly in a bath of their blood. More than 100,000 of the subjects of the King were butchered and many times that number died from wounds or privation. Then 150,000 living victims of Asoka were deported from their lands into slavery or starvation. Asoka was now supreme. He was master of nearly all India and Afghanistan. Most conquerors justify the hideous cruelty and criminality of war by the results. Alexander, Caesar, Charlemagne, Napoleon, and many others stressed how their conquests served humanity by breaking down barriers of race and frontier, by uniting areas that had been inimical to one another, under one flag. British imperialists of the eighteenth and nineteenth centuries used similar excuses for mass murders, which under the name of war, were accepted as legal and respectable and even had the endorsement of bishops. However, Asoka started feeling ashamed of himself and his actions before seeing the end of the horrors he had begun.

Of the prevailing religions of India at the time, only one had the courage to be unequivocally opposed to war and violence. The Buddhist monks in their yellow robes and the mild Buddhist laymen, their minds uncontaminated by the noxious fever of war, would have condemned the murderous aggressiveness of Asoka and would have quoted the Buddhist dictum that "Victory breeds hatred, for the conquered is unhappy." Those who persecuted or abused these Buddhists for their "disloyalty" to the emperor would have been astonished and puzzled by their reactions. For the Buddhists were governed by the advice of the Exalted One who had told a disciple, "If anyone abuses, strikes, stones, or beats you, brush aside worldly desires to retaliate and take this vow: 'My heart won't waver. I won't utter an evil word. I shall remain compassionate, soft-hearted, and without resentment.'" These Buddhists not only condemned violent acts towards men; they also opposed any ill-treatment or misuse of animals. In their gentleness and love of all created things they literally, "wouldn't even hurt a fly." How the ordinary subjects of the Emperor Asoka must have laughed at them for their soft hearts. The merriment would have resembled that of men who jeer at the kindly folk who protest against vivisection and the confinement of animals in space rockets and against all other callous sacrifices of defenseless living creatures on the altars of "science." Thus Asoka must have been an extraordinary man to humble himself to listen to the Buddhists and to reflect upon their message. When this message is received, fully understood and accepted, it permeates every cell of the brain. So before the war on Kalinga was over, the emperor was sensitized to its horrors. With the peace, the full tide of remorse swept over him. He saw how cruelly and uselessly he had added to the suffering of the world. Now he became fully a Buddhist.

The extent of the accomplishments of Asoka, the Buddhist, would not be known today were it not for some 5,000 words of inscriptions that he had carved on pillars, on rocks, and in caves throughout his empire. Thirty-five of these inscriptions still exist. Indeed, it was not until 1837 that a scholar named Prinsep succeeded in mastering the deep mystery of Asoka's language and translating one. In his stories on stone Asoka told how the horrors of war and conquest had led him to repent and to dedicate his life to moral conquest through religion. The inscriptions contain Buddhist rules for the laity. They explain the meaning of this religion. They reveal what Asoka accomplished for social welfare in his empire and how his abundant kindness and charity were showered on animals as well as on men. Then missionaries sent by Asoka converted Ceylon to Buddhism. Others went to Burma, to Syria, Egypt, Cyrene, Macedonia, and Epirus. These acts were the foundation of Asoka's greatness—not the "triumph" of his bloody conquests. So from generation to generation, tales of the glory of Asoka, man of peace, were in Asia handed down from parents to children. "If a man's fame," wrote Koppen, "can be measured by the number of hearts who revere his memory, by the number of lips who mentioned and still mention him with honour, Asoka is more famous than Charlemagne or Caesar." And H. G. Wells called him, "Asoka, greatest of kings."

This unique conqueror left upon one rock a confession for the sin of his conquest. He expressed his remorse for the sufferings he caused by inflicting such terrible losses on the enemy and such grief among those who were bereaved. He told of the mental agony that had led him to reform his life and to put the Teaching into practice. "What does the Teaching include?" asked Asoka in another inscription. "It includes an absence of self-indulgence, many good actions, kindness, generosity, truthfulness, and purity." On the borders of Asoka's empire were tribes he had never conquered. To them he dedicated an inscription saying, "The king desires they should have no fear of me and trust me. To them I wish not sorrow but happiness." He was an ardent, dedicated convert to Buddhism, yet he was completely without intolerance of the other faiths that flourished in his empire. "His majesty," wrote the emperor, "wishes that peoples of diverse sects should live in all places. For surely they all stand for control of passion and for the pure heart." And also, "Whoever praises his own sect and for its glorification condemns the faiths of others thereby more gravely injures his own." Asoka recorded that "All men are my children. And just as I wish my children every kind of prosperity and happiness, in this world and the next, so do I wish for all men." As for animals, he wrote that "In various ways I have been endowed with spiritual insight, and for two-footed and four-footed creatures, for birds and fishes, I have ordered many kindnesses and respect for their lives." More records reveal Asoka's gradual introduction of vegetarianism into his domains. There was a decree forbidding the slaughter of numerous animals and birds in addition to "all four-footed beasts which are neither utilized nor eaten." Daily in Asoka's palaces many animals had been slaughtered to provide curries for himself, his family and courtiers. Then he commanded that only three creatures be thus killed. These were to be two peacocks and one antelope. Eventually all slaughter for food or any other purpose was forbidden. Hunting for pleasure also ceased.

Military exercises, court entertainments, and sport were cast aside by the Emperor Asoka in his passion for the expansion of Buddhism. He went thousands of miles through India on pious tours. Arriving in a city or village with his entourage, Asoka would ask to meet religious leaders of all sects. He would also gather simple country folk around him to hear and to discuss the teaching of the Buddha. He organized or encouraged great and elaborate processions of witness. There arose on his instructions hundreds of monasteries. Places of special importance in the life story of the Buddha were marked by splendid memorials, and the emperor's subjects were encouraged to make pilgrimages to them. A favorite spot of the pilgrims was Lumbini Park, where Asoka had erected a large pillar inscribed with the words, "Here the Venerable One was born." The emperor built hospitals for men—and animals. He is credited with having started the profession of veterinary surgery. And near the hospitals for men and animals were established gardens for the cultivation of healing herbs. At intervals along the long, dusty roads of India were erected rest houses "for the comfort of man and beast." These were set in gardens of shady trees and flowers. A pioneer educationalist, Asoka urged Buddhist monks to raise the national level of instruction and, in their own religious studies, to submit their scriptures to what we call today "higher criticism." He championed and financially supported education for women. His reign lasted twenty-eight years—years of happiness and hope for the Indian sub-continent. Yet the splendor of this Buddhist Utopia was gradually to fade after Asoka's death.

Back came the caste-ridden influence of the Brahmins and the many uncomfortable superstitions of the Hindus. Buddhism was to fade from most of India; but thanks to Asoka the seeds of the Faith had been scattered in other lands, to grow and to bloom.

The most glorious flowering of Asoka's zeal in spreading the Buddha's message was in Ceylon. The message was carried by the monk Mahinda, who was either the son or the younger brother of the emperor. A man of infinite charm and eloquence, Mahinda had been twelve years a member of the Order when he was commanded to start on this, one of the most successful missions of history. The decision to send Mahinda was made by Asoka during a great Buddhist council in Patna. At almost the same time two monks, Sona and Uttara, carried the gospel to Burma. Mahinda set sail with cordial and elaborate documents of introduction from Asoka to Tissa, king of Ceylon. A dramatic meeting between monk and king was arranged in the scenic grandeur of Missaka Mountain. Before the assembled king and court Mahinda preached a long sermon on the Teaching. It was a practical sermon; it reasoned that the application of the Teaching in day-to-day life could bring to them all peace and equanimity. King Tissa and his retinue were converted and vowed to spread the Buddha's doctrines throughout the island. The king founded a large monastery and also in commemoration of his conversion built the Thuparama Dagoba or *stupa,* an architectural gem that still exists at Anuradhapura. Soon women relatives of King Tissa were demanding to become nuns. Mahinda appealed to his sister Sanghamitta, a member of the female Order in India, to hurry to his side in Ceylon. Quickly Sanghamitta with some of her sister nuns crossed to the island. With her she brought a branch of the historic Bodhi-tree under which the Buddha sat when he gained Enlightenment. The branch was planted at King Tissa's magnificent capital of Anuradhapura. And today it is claimed that a Bodhi-tree still there grew from that branch brought by Sanghamitta.

Ceylon is the country where the Buddhist Scriptures were first put into writing. This was done in 80 B.C. in the reign of King Vattagamani. What is less important, Ceylon is a land where religious relics and their veneration add to the fervor of the Buddhists. One precious relic is claimed to be a tooth of the Buddha. It is housed now in Kandy in the Temple of the Holy Tooth. In 1957 I visited this temple and was led into a "Holy of Holies" where the sacred tooth was to be exhibited to me. My guide told me that first I must hand over a sum of money for charity. I refused because this proposed commercial transaction seemed so inimical to the true spirit of Buddhism. So I never saw the tooth and, anyhow, I doubt its authenticity. Buddhism is so free that there is nothing to prevent any impostor from donning a yellow robe and calling himself a monk. In Ceylon, alas, the number of unscrupulous men who wear the Robe yet live contrary to the teachings of the Buddha has sadly increased in recent years. Thus the rabble-rousing activities of political "monks" and the dastardly assassination in 1959 of a Prime Minister. Worthier of veneration are the many, many ordinary Singhalese—both laymen and monks—who in their gentleness and sweetness enshrine the teaching that long ago Mahinda brought to their country. The loveliness of such characters has long been the wonder of Western visitors. There was the British seaman Robert Knox, held eighteen years in Ceylon as a prisoner in the seventeenth century. He wrote: "'Take a ploughman from the plough and wash off his dirt, and he is fit to rule a kingdom' was spoken of the people of Ceylon because of the civility, understanding, and gravity of the poorest among them. Their ordinary ploughmen and husbandmen do speak eloquently, and there is no difference between the ability of speech of a countryman and a courtier." Then there was Bishop R. S. Copleston who, in a critical but brilliant study of Buddhism in Ceylon, generously admitted: "I can heartily say that there are individuals who, as Buddhists, are seeking a good example, and doing their best to teach others what is good. Such ought not to be offended if I reckon them rather as friends of Christianity than as opponents."

6 MEDITATION

Meditation is becoming a fashionable craze among cliques of men and women who have plenty of time to spare, in Los Angeles, New York, London, and Paris. The most popular method being studied is that of Japan's Zen school, where complete enlightenment and comprehension of Reality is said to overwhelm a student suddenly when he or she is pondering upon what, to the reason, seems to be an imponderable riddle set by the teacher. I have superficially examined Zen in Japan, whose experts unkindly hint that the Zen enthusiasts of the West misunderstand the meditative practices and so make fools of themselves. Zen in Japan impressed me, but it should not be played as a kind of sport by Westerners of highly nervous or hysterical temperament. I am in this book concentrating upon Theravada Buddhism—but even so, I must warn against Western novices trying to throw themselves, without sufficient preparation, into the meditative "trances" of the trained monks of Burma, Thailand, and Ceylon. When I was last in Thailand, a young Briton who had taken the Robe was hustled back to England with a nervous breakdown. Against the advice of his teachers he had been too eager. Far from improving his mind, immoderate "meditation" had filled it with crazy illusions. This was not a solitary case. I was told of Englishwomen who could be called really silly. They arrived in Thailand's hot, steamy climate and then dedicated themselves to fasting, rigid self-disciplines, and non-stop meditation that quickly made them ill. The British Buddhist Society will not, indeed, accept anyone into its more rigid meditation classes without first investigating his or her suitability, physically and mentally. Thus, for the novice, I recommend the simple meditation exercises that follow. Then there will be no danger of saintly zeal being transformed into a mania. Alexander Pope warned us that,

For virtue's self may too much zeal be bad,
The worst of madness is a saint run mad.

I shall be unpopular among many Buddhists of the West for these introductory remarks upon meditation; for I am flying into the face of a popular cult and a craze. Nevertheless I emphasize that meditative practices are aids on the path to self-realization and are not the Path itself. Certainly they are not the most important duty of the Buddhist. Indeed, the pursuit of ecstasy in meditation can become a dangerous self-indulgence.

Now let us consider techniques of simple meditation. We must first be clear in our minds why we wish to meditate. "Cease to do evil; learn to do good; cleanse your own heart; this is the teaching of the Buddha." Well, meditation or concentration is a method of cleansing our hearts and minds so that, in a state of serenity, we may truly apprehend the true and the real. Day and night, in our sleeping and in our wakefulness, our mind is in a turmoil of thoughts, emotions, desires, loves, worries, and hatreds. While we sleep, the mind, in a subconscious state, runs wild in surging torrents of thoughts and dreams, a few of which we sometimes recollect on our awakening. Most of us experience the same kind of mental condition as we emerge from sleep into wakefulness. We feel ourselves leaving a whirl of thoughts and dreams, many ridiculous and illogical. "I had such a silly dream," we sometimes say, trying without success to recall all the details. Psychologists say that the average person has many dreams in a night, but on waking may not remember one of them. Then thought in the subconscious is continuous, a churning mass of problems, memories, and fears. When we get up in the morning our minds continue their mad, undisciplined wanderings. A superbly realistic picture of the eddies of thought and emotion in one individual is drawn by James Joyce in *Ulysses*. In a short period of time it ranges from Heaven to the toilet. Now analyze the working of your own mind when you rise in the morning. You think of the problems of the coming day, probably with some fear and misgiving. You recall old grudges and old hates and long to exact vengeance. There are desires for the attainment of ambition, for money and for popularity. Sensual thoughts sweep in; thoughts of food and sex and physical comfort. There come fears for the future, regrets for the past. Curiosity arises concerning what will be in the newspapers and what the radio news bulletin will contain. Thus the stream of thought and emotion moves onward. It is as if our mind were the lobby of a busy hotel, with people chattering and coming and going; or like a railroad station with passengers (our thoughts) arriving and departing amid rush and noise. Rarely is the mind of the average person clear and tidy.

Rarely is it in a condition to be able to think rationally and to make logical decisions. The average mind is too crowded with invading thoughts and emotions which dance around in useless confusion. This is a condition where the Right Concentration of Buddhism will help.

When you leave your bed in the morning, sit upright but comfortably in a chair. If your limbs are sufficiently youthful and elastic you may prefer to squat on the floor with legs crossed, like a meditating Asian; but not many Westerners feel comfortable in this posture. Clasp your hands, or rest them apart on your knees; it does not matter which. Breathe slowly, but not abnormally. If you have read complicated advice on posture and breathing in meditation, forget all about it for the present. Too many so-called Aids to Meditation read like advice to budding acrobats and physical contortionists. The novice must be himself, not an amateur Yogi. Now when you are comfortable and settled, fix your eyes on some object in the room. But if a steady stare at a single thing strains your eyes, close them and concentrate upon an object in your imagination. Suppose your chosen object is a white cup. You try to concentrate all your mind on this cup, to think of nothing else whatsoever. At first this proves difficult. Thoughts appear from nowhere and interfere with the attention the mind is trying to devote to the cup. These thoughts may be about the coming day, or they may concern some irrelevant memories or may be concerned with some noise inside or outside the house. When these mental gatecrashers try to come between yourself and the cup, drive them away by intensified concentration on the cup. As you look at this object (in reality or in your imagination) keep the invading thoughts at bay by repeating the words "Cup, cup, cup." At last your mind is aware of nothing but the white cup. All thoughts and fears and desires have gone. Then even the cup disappears from the consciousness and there is ineffable peace. Without all the thoughts and emotions, the mind seems to be all crystal clarity, like a pool of cool, clean water, like a polished mirror. What was a cluttered junk room of dusty, greedy ideas has become cleared, swept, and clean. Although there is no conscious thought, the mind seems to obtain an understanding of a Reality that transcends thought. This cannot be called a mystical experience because it seems so solid and so real. It is like being taken upon a mountain and seeing for the first time the whole terrain of a country from the single vantage point. Before we knew this country only in part, only in separated localities. Now, in one glance we see all in its grandeur and glory.

In this state it is easy to descend again to thought. But now it is possible to concentrate upon one theme in absolute clarity without the intrusion of unwanted ideas and emotions. Problems that have appeared insoluble at ordinary times become, in this condition of concentration, really simple. The Four Noble Truths, the Three Signs of Being, and other Buddhist teachings which may have seemed puzzling are, in the state of concentration, completely understood. All through this experience there is a feeling of light, of gladness, of peace. Then comes an impulse to return to the workaday world from the splendor of the mountain. You rise from your chair or from the floor. You are back in the ugly, stormy world of form and desire. But you are better for your experience. You feel less hatred, less fear. You think more clearly. There has been no time for dust to settle again on the mirror of your mind. All the intruders of thought that were driven out have not yet started to try to get back. You still see the world and its people as they really are and, as a consequence, you are more loving and more tolerant. Then how long did the concentration last for such wonders to be achieved? Anything from five minutes to half an hour. No doubt you are incredulous. But try it and see for yourself. Do not expect effective results on your first effort. It may take as many as ten sessions of concentration before you succeed in banishing all interrupting thoughts and winning your way to what is best described as Reality. But it is not so difficult. As I told you in the second chapter, many young people of Asia follow this simple technique of Right Concentration with success.

Anyone who tries to use Concentration and Meditation for material motives is a bad Buddhist and the law of Kamma (or cause) will eventually make him pay for his badness. Nevertheless it is certain that Buddhist Mindfulness and Concentration and general mind-training techniques produce an alertness and insight that must, rightly or wrongly, advance the layman in his worldly career. He learns "single-pointedness" of mind, to see problems objectively, to read character. What is more, Buddhist mind training creates in men and women a dignity and charm that attract admiration and loyalty. The popular volume *Concentration and Meditation*, published by the British Buddhist Society, states: "This poise of mind, this 'inner stillness and heart's quietude,' begets an immense, unmoving dignity, from which in turn is born in others a profound respect for the one who displays it, with consequent inquiries as to the philosophy which gave it birth. Common enough in the East, it is in the West so rare that it can almost be described as the hallmark of the meditator."

What prayer is to the Christian and the Moslem, meditation is to the Buddhist. Some Buddhist critics say that the supplications of prayer are self-seeking and egotistical. Dr. S. Radhakrishnan goes to the extreme of charging that "Prayer takes the character of private communications, selfish bargaining with God." He adds, "It seeks for objects of earthly ambitions and inflames the sense of self. Meditation on the other hand is self-change. It is the reconditioning of the soul, the transforming of its animal inheritance and social heredity." Yet the first meditations of Buddhism have been described by Christian scholars as "essentially Christian." These meditations are what Buddhists call the Four Illimitable Sublime Moods—Love, Compassion, Joy, and Serenity.

The Buddhist meditating on *Love* imagines the happiness that would be his if his nature knew no sorrow, anger, or temptation. Then he wishes such happiness to all people, friends and enemies. As the Buddhist sends out these thoughts of love to all beings, he increasingly feels his oneness with all creation and he realizes the folly of belief in a separate "self."

In the meditation on *Compassion* the Buddhist thinks of all who suffer and sorrow; he identifies himself with them. He tries to imagine the depths of their pain, and is stirred by thoughts of sympathy and pity. These make him intent upon relieving suffering at all times, wherever he may find it. The meditation brings clearly to him the serious significance of the first two of the Three Signs of Being—Sorrow and Impermanence.

The Buddhist next meditates on *Joy* by "rejoicing with those who rejoice." He thinks of those who prosper, who celebrate, who laugh and sing. Their good fortune fills him with joy. He wishes happiness to all beings. Again there is identification between this Buddhist and laughing children, singing birds, and gambolling animals. Again his sense of identity vanishes. His feelings of happiness and celebration give balance to his character, prevent him from making religion an excuse for dreariness, and destroy any tendency to become a killjoy.

In the last three meditations the Buddhist loved, mourned, and rejoiced with mankind and all other living beings. Now in the fourth meditation—on *Serenity*—he brings back his mind to calm and unperturbed detachment. This idea of Serenity is expressed by the Buddhist Ceylonese schoolchildren in the recitation of these lines:

Just as a compact, solid rock
Stands immobile in the hurricane,
Even so, amidst all praise and blame
The truly wise are shaken not.

The Buddhist is unshaken amidst all the worldly "opposites," such as good and evil, wealth and poverty, love and hate, youth and age. All are viewed calmly and objectively. In his meditation he sees himself in the storms and contradictions of life, but he remains cool, serene, and gracious. The mood can be compared with that of the Greek and Roman Stoics. In a similar spirit did Epictetus and Marcus Aurelius accept the relentless operation of cause and effect.

A critic is justified in asking, "But what good is achieved for anybody in such meditations? When in the contemplation of *Love* the Buddhist directs his affectionate thoughts to all quarters of the earth, do they really go there and have they any beneficial effects?" We believe that good thoughts have force because they build good Kamma (see Chapter Three). However, we do not know whether we can dispatch them like cablegrams to reach the minds of people far away. Suppose I directed thoughts of joy from a New England township to the people of Madagascar. Would they feel a sense of buoyancy in response? We do not know. Millions of Christians, with kind and loving thoughts, pray every Sunday for the welfare of the President of the United States in churches in every state of the Union. Thus if thoughts were creative forces that could be aimed towards any individual person, the President would be a very happy man. Yet I doubt whether the President is happier than many an obscure person who has only two or three relatives or friends to make him the object of kindly thoughts or prayers. The effectiveness of telepathy, despite the claims of Dr. J. B. Rhine, of Duke University, is still a subject of controversy. However, what we can be certain of is that the Four Illimitable Sublime Moods do have a marvellous effect upon the man or woman who meditates upon them. Perhaps psychologists would call it the power of suggestion—but those who meditate upon loving-kindness become kindlier and those who place themselves in the meditative mood of compassion become more sympathetic with suffering. Likewise, concentrated thoughts upon joy give the thinker a happier disposition, while concentration upon serenity develops a serene character. These and other reflections, whether in formal daily meditation or amid workaday activities, help towards building character and sweetness of disposition. The Four Illimitable Sublime Moods need not, indeed, be confined to the privacy of one's room. They may be cultivated during a bus journey or while waiting to keep an appointment or during a few free moments in the lunch hour or during a Sunday afternoon walk. Never forget one of the greatest of all Buddhist truths—that we are made by our thoughts.

Another meditation originated by the Buddha is on the Impurities of the Body. This is a meditation often evaded by numerous Western Buddhists as "not quite nice." In fact, some modern commentators have dismissed it as unsuited to this day and age. This attitude is but a cowardly escape from Buddhist realism. The meditation on the Impurities is useful because it makes us realize more fully not only the impermanence of our bodies but also their worthlessness as compounds of perishable matter. The meditation also makes us more fully understand the doctrine of Non-self. We are made in the image of no god. There are repulsive qualities about us all that should keep us humble. In the Meditation on the Impurities the Buddhist "looks at his body from the soles of his feet to the top of his head. He sees it as a thing enclosed by skin, with mixed impure contents." Then the Buddhist says: "This body of mine consists of hairs of the head, hair of the body, nails, teeth, skin; flesh, sinews, bones, marrow; kidneys, heart, liver, tissue; spleen, lungs, stomach, bowels; intestines, excrement, bile, phlegm; matter, blood, sweat, fat; tears, serum, saliva, mucus; lubricants and urine." Still more realistic, the Buddha suggested a Meditation on Death and Bodily Decay. He said, "A brother might imagine a corpse flung into a charnel-field. It is being devoured by birds of prey, by dogs, jackals and worms. . . . He sees bones scattered everywhere and he compares his own body with these and thinks, 'Here is the nature of my own body.' "

Buddhism, like Yoga, has breathing exercises that it links with meditation and concentration. Most of these, if attempted by a beginner, need the watchful instruction of a teacher. Ignorant and violent breathing experiments can produce hysteria. From these may also come a state of self-hypnosis that is likely to be mistaken for religious ecstasy.

Soon I shall tell you what I observed in a Burmese retreat where many were practicing advanced concentration on respiration. Meanwhile here are a few remarks regarding a simple and harmless method of breathing in concentration. Everybody knows that deep rhythmic breathing has a calming effect upon mind and emotions. Thus you may, with benefit, try this:

Take a deep breath through the nose; then exhale and, in your imagination, count one. Breathe in and count two. Exhale and count three. Breathe in and count four—and so on to ten or fifteen. Always you must concentrate upon the breathing functions, keeping all other thoughts from your mind. Gradually this exercise will you give a feeling of profound peace, of detachment from the material world. With practice this form of concentration may be lengthened and it won't be necessary to count. You will inhale and exhale, holding your breath before and after, without conscious effort. And into the infinite calm of your mind may come a comprehension of Reality beyond the range of normal thought.

The meditation of the Buddhist is closest to Christian prayer when he pours out his highest desires. But whereas the Christian cries—for example—"Make me honest and truthful," in supplication to his God, the Buddhist cries, in the form of a wish, "May I be honest and truthful." Buddhists, alone or in congregation, will often recite their many aspirations in this fashion. "May I be loving and compassionate to all beings; may I be patient and forgive the wrongs of others; may I be pure and virtuous. . . ." Surely these wishes have a creative quality that gives the Buddhist the will and the power to attain.

In higher meditation there is a systematic procedure

which, it is claimed, will give the Buddhist supreme, all comprehensive, wisdom and insight. But intense concentration and self-absorption are needed. Here is an effort of which only fully dedicated monks would be capable. This road to supreme wisdom is reached in four Stages of Meditation or the Four Jhanas (Pali). In the First Stage the monk devotes his mind to reasoning on some religious subject. In the Second Stage the monk's concentration gives his mind clarity, and reason becomes replaced by pure intuition. Then in the Third Stage the subject of his thought and intuition fades away. Now the monk is filled with a sense of eternal joy. Lastly, in the Fourth Stage, ecstasy passes, to be replaced by "a purity of equanimity and mindfulness, devoid of either joy or sorrow." This indeed must be close to the peace of Nibbana.

The Four Jhanas are not for Western laymen. Such intense concentration and meditation are the gift of only a few and come only after much striving. Yet in simple meditation, or in simple concentration, most of us may at times obtain a glimpse of the eternal Reality. This ability and its results have never been so well expressed as by Friedrich von Schelling, the nineteenth-century German philosopher of Idealism. In his *Philosophical Letters Upon Dogmatism and Criticism* he wrote, "In all of us there dwells a secret marvellous power of freeing ourselves from the changes of time, of withdrawing to our secret selves away from external things, and so discovering to ourselves the eternal in us in the form of unchangeability. This presentation of ourselves to ourselves is the most truly personal experience, upon which depends everything that we know of the suprasensual world. This presentation shows us for the first time what real existence is, whilst all else only appears to be. It differs from every presentation of the sense in its perfect freedom, whilst all other presentations are bound, being overweighted by the burden of the object. This intellectual presentation occurs when we cease to be our own object, when, withdrawing into ourselves, the perceiving image merges into the self-perceived. At that moment we annihilate time and duration of time. We are no longer in time, but time, or rather eternity itself (the timeless), is in us. The eternal world is no longer an object for us, but is lost in us."

Several years ago I was a guest of the monks at the famous Thathana Yeiktha (Meditation Center) near Rangoon in Burma. I failed to make the most of the opportunities offered me there for the study of meditation. Nevertheless my experiences are still vivid in my memory. They would have astounded some of those Western Buddhists who insist that absolute silence is necessary for successful meditation. Thathana Yeiktha is a point of attraction for monks in all parts of the Buddhist world. They come there to receive training in the meditative system of its principal, a monk named Mahasi Sayadaw. His system is hard and intensive. If practised diligently it will lead quickly to "enlightenment," according to the claims and testimony of many Buddhists. Laymen are also admitted to Thathana Yeiktha for Mahasi Sayadaw's mind-training. I drove to Thathana Yeiktha from Rangoon expecting to find monastic peace. Leaving my car I walked through its gilded gates to be welcomed cordially by the monks. They conducted me to my cell, with its rough wooden table and hard wooden bed; they suggested that I should rest there awhile in "silence and peace." The noise became excruciating. In the grounds were scores of stray dogs who had settled in the Meditation Center to be fed by the monks with their reverence for all life. The dogs barked and howled unceasingly. Then huge crows made the grounds their center too. They made a big noise as they glided low and settled on the trees and buildings. The road outside Thathana Yeiktha leads to Rangoon Airport. All day and far into the night the noise of the traffic could be heard. Immediately outside Thathana Yeiktha was a kind of market with open-air stalls and refreshment bars. The crowds around these added to the general din. Later I ceased to rest in "silence and peace" and walked the paths that run alongside the monks' cells. I gazed through open doors into some of the cells. There squatted monks lost and transfixed in meditation. Others walked with slow, regular steps up and down paths and the grounds. They saw nothing, they heard nothing. Amid the barking of dogs, cawing of crows, and other noises they moved in a mental world where all was silent. They were impressive examples of true Mindfulness. In those days I was boorish in my curiosity. Passing several meditative monks I addressed each loudly, asking how he was or remarking upon the sweaty heat of the day. None moved an eyelid or showed any indication of having seen or heard me.

Mahasi Sayadaw prescribed two exercises in particular as speedy methods of apprehending Reality through mental concentration. In one, the monk had to walk up and down keeping closest attention to the movement of his feet. In his mind he had to repeat precisely the rise and the fall of the feet in the walk. In a second exercise the monk sat with legs crossed, watched the movement of his stomach in breathing, its rise and fall. All other thoughts had to be excluded, just as we would have to exclude them in the simpler exercise of concentrating on a cup. Mahasi Sayadaw's students did this hour after hour, day after day.

The Sayadaw lived in a small house just inside the grounds of Thathana Yeiktha. There he spent hours in meditation and study, and giving personal advice to his students. I visited the monk with an interpreter who had advised me to kneel and bow three times in his presence. Mahasi Sayadaw sat cross-legged on a wicker chair when I and the interpreter entered his long reception room. Following the instructions and example of my interpreter I knelt and then bowed my head to the floor three times. The sight of the monk on his "throne" and my movements in showing him respect seemed so weird that suddenly I burst out laughing. In shame at my rudeness I looked up at the Sayadaw. He was smiling; and his smile slowly became a ripple of laughter. I tried to squat cross-legged on the floor, but failed because my limbs lacked the necessary litheness. Mahasi Sayadaw smiled again. Through the interpreter we joked about the difficulties that Westerners suffer in trying to be Eastern. Then we had a more serious conversation upon Buddhism and upon Christianity. I was no Buddhist at that time, but even the presence of Mahasi Sayadaw filled me with respect and awe. My guess was that he was in his late fifties, yet he had on his unlined face a look of the childlike purity that wholehearted devotion to Buddhism is said to give. I remember thinking that I had never before met anybody whose personality and appearance so pervaded the atmosphere with beauty and peace. Later, when telling a friend about the overwhelming impression that the famous monk made upon me, I remarked that "Jesus Christ must have been like that."

Finally—and this is important—Theravada Buddhism does not regard meditation or mind-training in general as a method of obtaining supernatural powers. It disapproves of self-important people who claim that their meditation exercises have given them unearthly ecstasies or the ability to perform miracles or, indeed, any kind of magic. It is true that monks in Tibet claim, from time to time, to be miracle workers. However, any Theravada monk who announces himself to have obtained supernatural powers is liable to dismissal from the Order. In the Roman Catholic Church a man's miracles may help to make him a saint; in Theravada Buddhism his miracles could bar him from sainthood. If meditation does give the Buddhist supernatural powers, then he must keep quiet about them. This attitude seems to be essentially healthy. Certainly it protects Buddhism from mountebanks.

7 A GUIDE TO LIFE

This, in the West, is a period of gigantic material and economic progress. The age of the fabulous multi-millionaire, with his vast estates and mansions, may be passing; but the average man and his wife have never been so prosperous. Even more remarkable, the fears for the future that once haunted the average American have been made all the more unnecessary by the spread of Social Security and sound pension schemes. This is the generation of the over-fed and the over-dressed; of lavish amusements that are presented in the home at the turn of a switch. It is the age in which hundreds of thousands can afford the thrills of foreign travel. College education—once for the select few—is now available to millions of young men and women. It is often boasted that everything in America has, with her amazing material progress, changed for the better. But what of man? Everything may appear happier; yet man himself is no happier. Today, as statistics prove, a bigger proportion of people than ever before worry themselves into insanity. Psychiatry has become a big business because of the fears of men and women that they are going mad. Anxiety about the catastrophic effects of a possible nuclear war has become a national obsession, resulting in incessant alarmist and unconstructive talk that disrupts the calm with which such a threat should be faced. Thousands of people of the West are, indeed, haunted by a sense of insecurity and inferiority. Yet this is no illusion. It is exactly what is the matter. Many of us *are* inferior and insecure because we have no convincing and workable religion or philosophy on which to base our lives with confidence. We are spiritually penniless in the midst of material plenty. Then why not give Buddhism a trial? But before I discuss why and how the practice of Buddhism can make happier and more confident men and women, let us reflect upon what others have said about it.

The great British scientist Thomas Huxley, in the Romanes Lecture of 1893, said: "Buddhism is a system which knows no God in the Western sense, which denies a soul to man and counts the belief in immortality a blunder, which refuses any efficacy to prayer and sacrifice, which bids men to look to nothing but their own efforts for salvation, which in its original purity knew nothing of the vows of obedience and never sought the aid of the secular arm, yet spread over a considerable portion of the world with marvellous rapidity, and is still the dominant creed of a large fraction of mankind." Discussing the Buddha as philosopher, Huxley said: "It is a remarkable indication of the subtlety of Indian speculation that Gotama should have seen deeper than the greatest of modern Idealists."

Schopenhauer, the German philosopher, said: "If I am to take the results of my philosophy as the standard of truth I should be obliged to concede to Buddhism the pre-eminence over the rest. In any case it must be a satisfaction to me to find my teaching in such close agreement with a religion professed by the majority of men. This agreement must be all the more satisfactory because in my philosophizing, I have certainly not been under its influence."

That outstanding psychologist the late Professor Carl Jung, of Zurich, wrote that "as a student of comparative religion, I believe that Buddhism is the most perfect one the world has ever seen. The philosophy of the Buddha, the theory of evolution and the law of Kamma were far superior to any other creed."

An eminent British psychiatrist, Dr. Graham Howe, has said: "To read a little Buddhism is to realize that the Buddhists knew, 2,500 years ago, far more about modern problems of psychology than they have been given credit for. They studied these problems long ago and found the answers also. We are now rediscovering the ancient wisdom of the East."

The great Pali scholar Dr. Rhys Davids was the son of a clergyman. He started translating the Buddhist scriptures into English with the plan of proving that Christianity was very superior to Buddhism. Instead Dr. Rhys Davids became a convinced Buddhist and testified: "I have examined every one of the great religions of the world, and in none of them have I found anything to surpass the beauty and comprehensiveness of the Four Noble Truths of the Buddha. I am content to shape my life according to that path."

Edward Conze, one of the greatest living Buddhist scholars and translators, has said: "Although one may originally be attracted by its remoteness, one can appreciate the real value of Buddhism only when one judges it by the result it produces in one's own life from day to day."

The late H. G. Wells, enthusiastically praising Buddhism

as an ethical system, added: "Over great areas of the world it still survives. It is possible that in contact with Western science, and inspired by the spirit of history, the original teaching of Gotama, revived and purified, may yet play a large part in human destiny."

Even though he would deny the truth of Buddhism, the French Christian writer René Grousset admits it has much to teach. Grousset says that "the Christian can admire without reservation the many human beauties that Buddhism brings to light. . . . Without perhaps looking for truth there, he will not forbid himself to draw lessons from it."

Writers of many generations have remarked upon an indefinable attractiveness about Buddhist personalities and Buddhist countries. Some attribute this to the benevolence that is born from the practice of Buddhist virtues. In his study of Buddhist benevolence, Hermann Oldenberg wrote: "Whoever bears benevolence within him possesses therein as it were a magical power; men and beasts, when he lets fall on them a ray of this power are thereby wondrously subdued and attracted."

In a Hibbert Lecture Professor Rhys Davids described a meeting in Ceylon with a monk who possessed this mysterious magnetism. "There was a strange light in his sunken eyes," said Davids. "There was an indescribable attraction about him, a simplicity, a high-mindedness, that filled me with reverence."

Prime Minister Nehru of India tells how in his youth he became fascinated by the story of the Buddha. Later in visiting Buddhist countries he felt that the purity of the doctrine had been too much overlaid by form and ceremonial. "But I saw much also that I liked," added Nehru. "There was an atmosphere of peaceful study and contemplation in some of the monasteries and the schools attached to them. There was a look of peace and calm on the faces of many of the monks, a dignity, a gentleness, an air of detachment and freedom from the cares of the world. Did all this accord with life today, or was it a mere escape from it? Could it not be fitted into life's ceaseless struggle and so tone down the vulgarity and acquisitiveness and violence that afflict us?" [1] Then in a moving comment on the calm beauty of images of the Buddha, Nehru has said: "The ages roll by and Buddha seems not far away after all; his voice whispers in our ears and tells us not to run away from the struggle, but calm-eyed, to face it, and to see in life even greater opportunity for growth and advancement."

In Victorian and Edwardian days many books were written on Buddhist countries that extolled Western culture and modernity and deplored Eastern "backwardness." However, it is remarkable how many authors of such books were persuaded by their personal observations to pay tribute to the effects of the Buddhist faith.

J. G. D. Campbell, a British official who lived for years in Siam (Thailand), in 1902 published a book entitled *Siam in the Twentieth Century*. In this he wrote: "There are not the awful chapters in the history of Buddhism which disfigure that of Christianity. Persecution is alien to the spirit of Buddhism, which is suffused with charity and gentleness. It is, indeed, in some ways refreshing to leave for a while the war of sects at home in order to sojourn in a land where religion is pervaded by the true spirit of—shall we call it Christian?—charity."

In 1897, Professor Maxwell Sommerville returned from a visit to Siam to his post at the University of Pennsylvania

[1] *The Discovery of India.*

to write a book, *Siam on the Neinan,* in which he said: "The paramount principles pervading the entire system of the Buddhist religion are self-abnegation, meditation and obedience to a code which any Christian might endorse: a code of morals which, if strictly observed in Christian countries, would elevate society to a higher standard than has been reached under all our boasted religious culture. That code is a garden of spiritual flowers whose odor is the beauty of holiness, and from which we will cull only so many as will give a fair idea of the chaste, honest, ennobling sentiments which are, and have been for centuries, distilled into the hearts and minds of a people whom American Christians designate as heathen."

H. Fielding Hall, who was in Burma as a soldier and official, learned to love its religion and the lovely characters it created.

In *The Soul of a People,* published in 1898, he wrote of Buddhism: "Surely this is a simple faith, the only belief that the world has known that is free from mystery and dogma, from ceremony and priestcraft; and to know that it is a beautiful faith you have but to look at its believers and be sure. If a people be contented in their faith, if they love it and exalt it, and are never ashamed of it, and if it exalts them and makes them happy, what greater testimony can you have than that?"

Soon after the Second World War, officers of the Troop Information and Education Section of the United States Army were asked to compile a handbook for its men then based in Korea. The officers "investigating" the Korean people were captivated by an attractiveness that seemed mysterious. That is, until the officers studied Korea's Buddhist background. Then, in their handbook, they wrote:

"Possibly, too, in that indefinable charm and affectionateness of manner which is found in the Korean people is to be seen an even clearer mark of the past influence of that Great Teacher (Buddha) who, whatever his faults and shortcomings, certainly laid supreme stress on gentleness and kindness to others."

So that is what Buddhism has done for other people. Now what can it do for ourselves? Is it really a philosophy that could bring order into our lives and sense into our rich yet chaotic Western civilization? Indeed it could; and there is abundant individual testimony to its swift effectiveness when once accepted and practiced.

"And as the erstwhile galley slave with ever fresh delight demonstrates the freedom of his limbs, so he who was formerly in the thrall of lust, hate, and error demonstrates with rapture ever renewed: 'I have comprehended. I am free.'"

Thus does Paul Dahlke convey to us the exultant feelings of the man whom Buddhism has liberated. His cares, worries, and fears—and hopes—fade into nothingness. So few of these had ever any reason for existence. They tortured him because he believed in the illusion called "self." He had been a slave of that illusion, cherishing the "self," safeguarding its "dignity" and yearning for immortality. He had also become chained to a host of conflicting desires that brought him suffering when they were not satisfied. Life was a madhouse of wanting, of hating, of lusting, of posing. To feel self-important is to be self-conscious. When he lost the illusions of the reality and sanctity of self, he lost self-consciousness with its painful and absurd complexes. The Buddhist convert persevered in loving all and hating none. Kindly feelings towards his enemies soothed his nerves and invigorated his body. For hatred is a disease which, according to modern theory, poisons the body and mind of the hater. Cultivation of the Buddhist virtues and abandonment of the idea of a sacrosanct self will transform an ugly personality into one of compelling attractiveness.

Buddhism is not the religion exclusively for the monk and ascetic, and meditating devotee on his last stage to Nibbana. Buddhism is also for the ordinary man, ordinary woman, and ordinary child who may have many hundreds of rebirths before the peace and perfection of Nibbana is obtained. In the words of Edward J. Thomas,[2] "The new Teaching was not merely a way of salvation for those who had come to feel the emptiness of all earthly pleasures. It was also a guide of life for those in the world, and it taught the duties of social life not merely as a means of accumulating merit but as a moral discipline. The Buddha expected ordinary people to strive to understand the Four Noble Truths and to model their lives on the Eightfold Path. He also gave practical suggestions for the guidance of the laity." Outstanding are what are known as the Buddhist Beatitudes. A Deva (or spirit) was said to have approached the Buddha and asked: [3]

Many gods and men, desirous of benefit
Have pondered and devised acts of blessedness:
Declare Thou, what is the greatest act of blessedness?

The Buddha answered:

Not to associate with fools
But to keep company with the wise;

[2] *The Life of the Buddha as Legend and History.*
[3] Translation from Pali text by Francis Story.

To pay honor to those who are worthy—
This is the greatest act of blessedness.

To dwell in a favorable place;
To have done good deeds in former lives;
To have a mind that is rightly directed—
This is the greatest act of blessedness.

To be possessed of learning and of skill,
With courtesy and perfect discipline,
And well-regulated speech—
This is the greatest act of blessedness.

The support of mother and father,
The cherishing of wife and children;
A livelihood free from complications—
This is the greatest act of blessedness.

Practising charity, living in righteousness;
Protecting one's relatives
And doing blameless deeds—
This is the greatest act of blessedness.

To cease and refrain from all wrongdoing;
To abstain from the intoxicants;
Vigilance in observing the Dhamma—
This is the greatest act of blessedness.

Having reverence and true humility,
Contentment and gratitude;
Hearing the Doctrine at due seasons—
This is the greatest act of blessedness.

Patience and pleasant speech,
Association with the holy Brotherhood;
Religious talk at times appropriate—
This is the greatest act of blessedness.

Self-discipline and chastity;
Perception of the Four Noble Truths,
And the attainment of Nibbana—
This is the greatest act of blessedness.

To have a mind unshaken
By the impact of worldly conditions,
Free from sorrow, undefiled, secure—
This is the greatest act of blessedness.

They who have accomplished such things
Cannot in any wise meet with defeat
But go in safety in all places—
Theirs is the greatest act of blessedness.

Now, getting down to details, here is the solution offered by Buddhism to outstanding problems and worries of life.

GENERAL UNHAPPINESS

To rid yourself of this, reduce to a minimum your cravings and your wants. Cultivate a splendid indifference to gain. Remember that everything is impermanent, everything is passing. Why desire what time will never allow you to keep? If you want nothing, then nothing can hurt you. "Whoso," wrote Paul Dahlke, "is also stripped of all desires —him neither man nor god can any more touch at all; he is become invincible, and because he has become invincible therefore he is without fear." Cultivate love for all creatures and never be offended by ill-treatment and rebuffs.

ILLNESS AND DEATH

Both will come, and both must be accepted with equanimity. According to modern psychological theory much mental stress is caused by refusal to face and accept life's realities. This stress, unless overcome, actually can cause grave physical illnesses. Certainly worry and despair over illness will make it worse. As for death, it is never to be feared by the pure in heart and action. Anyhow we are all part of the living cosmos and have no individual self to die. The survival of evil qualities from our evil actions may cause us to suffer in a reborn body. But so long as we acquire merit now by living virtuously, we can face the future with confidence. We must verily face it bravely and realistically as Buddhism offers no "savior" upon whom to cast our burdens and to rescue us from the consequences of our wrong actions. We must constantly remind ourselves of the Buddha's command, "Be ye refuges and islands unto yourselves." Buddhists do not go into paroxysms of grief and mourning over the deaths of relatives and friends. There can be no halting of the wheel of circumstance. When a man dies and the fruits of his conduct pass into a new being, those left behind bear their bereavement with the calm that understanding creates.

HATRED, MALICE, AND JEALOUSY

"For not by hate is hate destroyed," said the Buddha, "but by love alone is hate destroyed. . . . Kindly thought is the best method of retaliation." Therefore the sincere Buddhist never sinks so low as to permit himself thoughts of hatred, malice, jealousy. He regards those who harm or dislike him with affectionate compassion and genuine forgiveness. When people are antagonistic towards you for no sensible reason, realize that their conduct is probably caused by their mental unbalance. Show goodwill in return and they may become aware of this unbalance and revert to equipoise.

Thoughts of affection can, with an effort of will, be made to replace thoughts of hate. And "to love those that hate you" will usually make them end their obsession and begin thinking kindly of you in return. Since the genuine Buddhist despises worldly standards of success and "superiority," he can never allow himself sentiments of jealousy. Hatred, malice, and jealousy cause their possessor physical harm too, and they sully our clean feeling of mental and moral purity. The *Dhammapada* expresses this feeling in the lines:

In the very bliss we dwell, those who hate not those who hate us;
Among men full of hate, we continue free of hate.

SHYNESS

The Buddhist is modest, but rarely shy or bashful. The philosophy of denial and renunciation surprisingly produces persons of strong self-confidence. We know that the Buddhist is taught to rely upon himself and not to lean upon dogma or to pin faith in the goodwill of an almighty Heavenly Father. But the absence of faith in such notions might surely make him a nervous person, full of feelings of insecurity and lacking self-confidence among his fellows. However, the secret of dispelling shyness and other offshoots of fear is to remind ourselves of the Buddhist teaching that there is no intrinsic "self." Then, if there is no independent "self" we have nothing to apologize for or to feel shy about! To be self-confident because we have no "self" reads like a foolish, self-contradictory statement. Nevertheless we should accept ourselves as a combination of aggregates, as a combination that is never permanent but always in the process of becoming. So when next you feel drifting towards nervousness or shyness, tell yourself, "There is no 'me' to be despised or to suffer, so I have nothing to be embarrassed about."

PRIDE AND SELF-IMPORTANCE

Once again we must think about the doctrine of non-self when pride is considered. What is pride but morbid worship of the so-called self? Then how can man be puffed with pride when he becomes aware that he has no "self"? We can never be happy and calm in mind if we waste effort and anxiety on pretending we are important. We shall then always be pained by offenses and snubs—real or imagined—from others. Vain and cruel is false dignity because it is an assumption of superiority over our fellows. Dignity is noble only when it is natural and unconscious; it has no association with self-pride. For example, there is genuine dignity in the Buddhist monk, and he regards pride and self-importance as among the great evils. Remember that pride and self-righteousness are two of the Ten Fetters. To avoid the disease of pride, ignore all worldly ideas of success and failure. The wise man will, in the words of the Tao Teh King, "aim at disinterestedness and maintain the utmost possible calm."

FAITH AND DOGMA

Buddhism is not an easy religion to practice. The Eightfold Path is beset with obstacles that need tenacious willpower to overcome. Even the Five Precepts mean a struggle if they are faithfully to be observed. But Buddhism does have the advantage of being without rigid creeds, without dogmas that baffle the reason yet demand acceptance. Doubt concerning the Teaching is one of Buddhism's Ten Fetters. But honest doubt is not looked upon as a sin. It is seen only as one of the factors delaying the development of character. The Buddha is no jealous God demanding blind faith and obedience. He was a man who pointed the way without claiming exclusive divinity or greatness.

One day, the disciple Sariputta, boasting to the Budda of his faith, said:

"I have such faith, Lord, that I believe there never has been, nor ever will be, nor ever is at present any other greater than thee, the Blessed One."

"So, Sariputta," was the reply, "of course you have known all the Buddhas of the past?"

"No, Lord."

"Then," continued the Buddha, "you know all the Buddhas of the future?"

"No, Lord."

"But at least you know me and have fully comprehended my mind?"

"Not even that, Lord."

"Then why, Sariputta, are your words so grand and sweeping?"

The Buddha asked the exclusive devotion of nobody. He asked nobody to abandon his religious creed. The Buddha could preach a sermon at a Brahmin's Sacred Fire yet not denounce his worship. He could receive Siha, the Jain, into Buddhism yet ask him to continue making donations to Jain monks. Thus you can become a Buddhist without execrating your former religious loyalties. You may practise Buddhism without feeling you must swallow a concatenation of dogma and creeds. You will not be expected to struggle to believe—but you will be expected to struggle to act. Then, by your actions, you will, willy-nilly, prove to yourself the truth of the Buddhist creed. Thus, in advice to his monk son Rahula, does the Buddha point to a course of effective action:

Practice kindliness, for thereby all hate will be abandoned.
Practice compassion, for thus will all vexation be abandoned.
Practice sympathy, for thereby will all aversion be abandoned.
Practice equanimity, for thereby will all repulsion be abandoned.
Meditate on the ugly and so will lust be abandoned.
Think about impermanence and then will self-pride be abandoned.

From such actions springs abounding faith.

WEALTH

Buddhism does not condemn wealth that is honestly earned. There are no outright condemnations of the rich man, as in the Christian Gospels and Epistles. Thus, in this Western system of free enterprise, the Buddhist does not have to face the embarrassing problem of the Christian in trying to justify even the honest accumulation of riches with the clear Gospel statement that it is easier for a camel to go through the eye of a needle than for a rich man to enter God's Kingdom.

In Buddhism the monk must abandon all material things. But the layman does himself no evil in achieving wealth, so long as this does not become a selfish obsession. "It is not life and wealth and power that enslave men," say the Buddhist Scriptures, "but the cleaving to life and wealth and power." And the rich man is expected to regard his wealth as a trust, with much of it devoted to the alleviation of suffering and of the poverty of others. However, wealth and its possession have no connection whatsoever with true happiness. For "worldly profit is fleeting and perishable, while religious profit is eternal and inexhaustible." The Buddha many times stressed that our happiness depends only upon our own minds and not upon external things.

WAR AND POLITICS

No man can be a genuine Buddhist and at the same time justify aggressive war and the violence of the bully. You will have gathered sufficient of Buddhism in this book to understand quite clearly that it is a religion of peace. The world likes to call the doctrine of non-violence "impossible" and "impractical." But in the opinion of William James, "If things are ever to move upward, someone must be ready to take the first step. . . . No one who is not willing to try charity and non-resistance, as the saint is always willing, can tell whether these methods will or will not succeed." Then the Buddhist's sentiments of love and goodwill for all men—and animals too—do not halt at any national frontier or ideological curtain. He has not faith that any political system as such, whether Communist or Democratic, can bring peace and happiness to mankind. First there must be a reformation in the character of individual man. Before the real Buddhist gets excited over the claims of any political party to create a better society, he strives to make his own character more worthy. He does not admire the man who dominates or conquers others nearly so much as he admires the man who conquers himself. He believes with the *Dhammapada* that "If one man conquer in battle a thousand men, and if another conquer himself, he is the greatest of conquerors. One's own self conquered is better than the conquest of all other people; not even a god could change into defeat the victory of a man who is self-controlled and always calm."

Buddhism is often called a religion of pacifism. And this

is true in the sense that Buddhists have never, unlike Christians and Moslems, waged so-called religious wars. But today (as in the past) there are many good Buddhists who, in defense of their families and homes against murderous aggression, would not refuse to take up arms. Probably the most peaceful, non-violent people in the world are the Buddhist Tibetans. Yet when Communist Chinese hordes invaded their country, they fought in its defense.

Perhaps, after reading this book, you may feel you would like to follow the principles of Buddhism in your own personal life. Then you might ask, "How do I become a Buddhist?" There is no compulsory initiation ceremony, although in some countries converts like formally to recite The Triple Refuge (page 31) and the Five Precepts (page 48) before a member of the Buddha's Order. There is no baptism or confirmation as in a Christian church. In fact a man or woman can become a Buddhist without making any declaration or taking any vow, or, indeed, telling anybody about it. All the convert has to do is to start basing his conduct on the Eightfold Path, the Five Precepts, and other teachings of the Buddha. Never need the Buddhist publicly renounce his former religious affiliation; and needlessly to criticize his former faith would be grossly ungrateful. All religions that believe in the spirit of love and forgiveness have the goodwill of the Buddhist. Indeed there is no reason why the Western Christian who becomes a Buddhist should not, in love and toleration, continue to support his former church and even to attend its services. Although unable any longer to recite its creeds, he can support anything that will encourage the practice of the exhortation to "Love thy neighbor as thyself." We may disbelieve much of the dogma of organized Christianity. Nevertheless many of its devoted leaders, past and present, demand our respect, as do also Christian art and other aspects of Christian life and culture. We can remain deeply conscious of the debt owed to Christian charitable, social, and medical work in countries all over the world, including those where Buddhism is the prevailing religion.

The Buddhist also respects the finer aspects of the faiths of Moslems and Jews and certainly of the Hindus. He also has understanding sympathy for the agnostic, and also for the atheist; why, Christian critics have accused Buddhism of being atheistic! Exclusiveness, narrowness, bigotry—none could live in the rarefied air of pure Buddhism. The Buddhist should not, however, expect the respect and toleration that he shows towards other faiths in the West to be reciprocated. Many Westerners regard a Buddhist as a crackpot or crank. This is because of their narrow intellectual upbringing during which all religions except Christianity are belittled, and because of the ridiculous picture of Buddhism given in popular fiction, journalism, and films. Frankly, a case could be made for blaming individual Western Buddhists for stimulating the scorn of the ignorant and misled masses for Buddhism. There are, alas, Western Buddhists who, in an inordinate passion for things Asian, show unconcealed and unjustifiable contempt for almost all aspects of our European and American religious and philosophical culture. There are also Western Buddhists who make a mystique of their faith by never discussing it without liberal use of Pali or Sanskrit phrases which, to the ears of ordinary folk, are gibberish. Pure Buddhism can be expressed clearly in English: it is not esoteric; it has no holy mysteries. Some Buddhists further baffle the ignorant by making too much fuss over their meditation and its methods; but I have already discussed this.

However sane and sensible he is in conversation and practice, the Buddhist convert in the West must resign himself to being laughed at and being regarded as an odd, eccentric character by persons of limited knowledge. On the other hand, the Buddhist convert will meet with respect and comradeship from others. There are now thousands of convinced Buddhists or students of Buddhism in America, Europe, and Australia. Many of these are united into societies. There is a constant interchange of magazines, speakers, and ideas between the Buddhist groups of America and those of Europe and Asia. For example, "The Golden Lotus," a simply produced mimeographed magazine published in Philadelphia, has a world circulation. There are an estimated 150,000 Buddhists in America (including its new states of Alaska and Hawaii), but most of these are of Japanese or Chinese extraction and belong to the Pure Land School. Study of Theravada Buddhism has become increasingly popular among Americans of European origin in the societies and the universities. In Washington, D.C., for instance, there is the flourishing "Washington Friends of Buddhism." There are also "Friends of Buddhism" groups in cities that include New York, Chicago, Philadelphia, and San Francisco. New York City has a Buddhist Academy for study and training. The biggest Buddhist organization in Europe is the Buddhist Society of Great Britain, with a fine headquarters and valuable library in London. This society was founded by Christmas Humphreys, a brilliant British lawyer and author. Then there is a World Fellowship of Buddhists that may one day have the same authority among Buddhists as the World Council of Churches has among Christians. Buddhist delegates from some thirty western and eastern nations have attended Asian conferences of the World Fellowship.

It was a poem published in 1879 that caused a sudden, dramatic upsurge in Western interest in Buddhism. This was "The Light of Asia," by Sir Edwin Arnold, a London journalist. An oriental scholar, Arnold had earlier been principal of the Sanskrit College in Poona, India. Some critics have sneered at Arnold's blank verse story of the Buddha as "poor poetry." Scholars have complained that the story is distorted and wanders from fact because Arnold obtained material from sources that were doubtful. Nevertheless, "The Light of Asia" swept the English-speaking world, made many converts and stimulated scholarly study of Buddhism. Sir Edwin Arnold was attacked by bigoted Christians for alleged idolization of the Buddha at the expense of Jesus Christ. He tried to make amends by telling the story of Jesus Christ in poetry in "The Light of the World." This was not nearly as successful as "The Light of Asia," probably because, in those days, the story of the Buddha was almost a complete novelty. Two other British scholars, Professor and Mrs. T. W. Rhys Davids, also made invaluable contributions to the elucidation of Buddhism. In 1881 this couple founded the Pali Text Society. This society is still introducing to the English-speaking world the vast Scriptures of the Theravada School in accurate and scholarly translation. Western comprehension of Buddhism also owes a deep debt to an American, Colonel H. S. Olcott, the founder and first president of the Theosophical Society, and author of a Buddhist Catechism of great clarity. The division of Buddhism into the Theravada, Mahayana, and other differing schools worried Olcott so much that in 1891 he strove concisely to outline the basic beliefs to which all might adhere. And at a congress in Madras, Buddhist leaders of Japan, Ceylon, Burma, and India accepted Olcott's "Fourteen Basic Buddhist Beliefs" as "a common platform upon which we can all agree."

Here are extracts from the statement of an American that Asians welcomed as a beautiful and clear expression of their essential unity:

Buddhists are taught to show the same tolerance, forbearance, and brotherly love to all men, without distinction; and an unswerving kindness towards the members of the animal kingdom.

The Universe was evolved, not created; and it functions according to law, not according to the caprice of any God.

The Buddha taught that ignorance produces desire, unsatisfied desire is the cause of rebirth, and rebirth the cause of sorrow. To get rid of sorrow, therefore, it is necessary to escape rebirth; to escape rebirth, it is necessary to extinguish desire; and to extinguish desire, it is necessary to destroy ignorance.

The dispersion of all this ignorance can be attained by the persevering practice of an all-embracing altruism in conduct, development of intelligence, wisdom in thought, and destruction of desire for the lower personal pleasures.

Right Meditation leads to spiritual enlightenment, or the development of that Buddha-like faculty which is latent in every man.

The essence of Buddhism as summed up by the Buddha himself is:

> To cease from all sin,
> To get virtue,
> To purify the heart.

The universe is subject to a natural causation known as "Kamma." The merits and demerits of a being in past existences determine his condition in the present one. Each man, therefore, has prepared the causes of the effects which he now experiences.

Buddhism discourages superstitious credulity. Gotama Buddha taught it to be the duty of a parent to have his child educated in science and literature. He also taught that no one should believe what is spoken by any sage, written in any book, or affirmed by tradition, unless it accord with reason.

Buddhism in the United States and, indeed, in other Western countries, is in debt also to the work of another American pioneer, Dr. Paul Carus, whose book *The Gospel of the Buddha* was first published in La Salle, Illinois, in 1894. Over one million copies have been sold of this charming work of narration and quotation from the Buddhist Scriptures. Then a more recent contributor to Buddhist studies was Dwight Goddard, compiler of *A Buddhist Bible.* This son of Worcester, Massachusetts, became deeply attracted to the message of the Buddha while a Christian missionary in China. Goddard founded an itinerant brotherhood called "The Followers of the Buddha." He died in Randolph, Vermont, in 1939 at the age of 78. His zeal inspired Mrs. Miriam Salanave, an Iowa-born woman, who until her death in San Francisco in 1943 worked ceaselessly to persuade American women to accept and spread Buddhist teachings which she had personally studied in Asia. A number of Americans have become Buddhist monks in Asian countries. Among them is Robert Clifton, now a wearer of the Robe in Malaya, after striving to further the cause of Buddhism in the United States.

And so, through the efforts of the Rhys Davidses, Colonel Olcott and other such pioneers, the seeds for the growth of Buddhism throughout the West were sown. An increasing number of men and women, bewildered by the material and ideological chaos of today, are finding that the teaching of the Buddha brings them back to sense and clarity, to serenity and peace. At the same time they are awakened to the adventure and the challenge of the Teaching as they recall his exhortation to labor on with diligence.

8 THE BUDDHA SPEAKS

The words of the Buddha, which I shall quote in this chapter, are from the Theravadin Canon, the most ancient record of his teachings. Tradition says that after the death of the Buddha a Council was convened; his teachings were recited by close followers and approved as authentic. The many thousands of words thus accepted by the First Council have the picturesque name of the *Tripitaka* or *The Three Baskets.* And each contains a variety of discourses or sermons (suttas).

Number One is the *Basket of Discipline* (*Vinaya Pitaka*). This concentrates mainly on the rules and regulations to be observed by the Order of Monks.

Number Two is the *Basket of Discourses* (*Sutta Pitaka*), chiefly containing sermons and talks given by the Buddha at various places to monks, laymen, and children.

Number Three is the *Basket of Ultimate Doctrines* (*Abhidhamma Pitaka*) which, profound and complex, contains an analysis of the Teaching and of Buddhist metaphysics. Some critics question whether all this is the direct teaching of the Buddha himself. They attribute much of it to scholarly monks seeking to develop metaphysical theories on which the Buddha had only lightly touched or even deliberately avoided.

This Theravadin Canon was handed down by word of mouth from generation to generation of monks for some five hundred years before finally being committed to writing. But many scholars have said that this fact does not necessarily make its accuracy the more questionable. For the monks were known to have been almost fanatically scrupulous in memorizing the Teaching and in reciting it "word perfect." To aid their memories they used in their narration a system of incessant repetition and often of versification. Thus translations from the Canon, with many repetitive phrases, at first read strangely. But when these repetitions are deleted there appears a rugged prose in which the Buddha, in his sermons and conversation, comes to life as does Jesus in the Gospels.

Now follow quotations directly attributed to the Buddha, and also from the famous, beloved Buddhist manual, the *Dhammapada*. While scholars regard the *Dhammapada* as an anthology, they say that much of its contents would have come from the Buddha himself.

HIS FIRST SERMON

Brethren, there are two extremes which he who has given up the world should avoid.

What are these two extremes? One extreme is a life devoted to pleasures and lusts. For such a life is degrading, sensual, vulgar, profitless, and ignoble. And the other extreme is a life devoted to self-mortification. This is painful, ignoble, and profitless.

By avoiding these two extremes, the Tathagata has obtained knowledge of the Middle Path, leading to calm, knowledge, insight, and Nibbana.

What is the Middle Path that leads to these gifts?

It is the Noble Eightfold Path consisting of right view, right resolution, right speech, right conduct, right livelihood, right effort, right mindfulness, right concentration.

This, brethren, is that Middle Path which brings knowledge, calm, insight, enlightenment, and Nibbana.

Now, brethren, here is the Noble Truth about suffering:

Birth is suffering, illness is suffering, and death is suffering. To be near things we hate and to be separated from the things we like is suffering; and not to get what we want is suffering. Then this body, with its five aggregates of grasping, is suffering.

Now here is the Noble Truth about the arising of suffering:

It starts with the craving that leads to birth. It is accompanied by sensual pleasures demanding satisfaction, now here and now there. That is to say, craving to be reborn or craving for the end of rebirth.

Then this is the Noble Truth concerning the cessation of suffering:

It is the complete and passionless abandonment of this craving and the release from this craving.

Now the way leading to the cessation of suffering is that of the Noble Eightfold Path. That is to say, right view, right resolution, right speech, right conduct, right livelihood, right effort, right mindfulness, right concentration.

With my realization of the Noble Truths there came to me vision, insight, understanding, and illumination. And as I possessed in perfect purity this understanding of the Noble

Truths, there came the realization that I had obtained supreme enlightenment in the world of men and gods.

Then knowledge and insight arose in me thus: "Sure is my release. This is my last birth. I shall not be born again."

Samyutta-Nikaya

NON-SELF

"The body, brethren, is selfless, for it is destructible. Nor do sensation, perception, the predispositions, and consciousness together form the self. For if this were so, then consciousness would also not be destructible.

"What do you think?" the Buddha asked the five converts to whom he was preaching. "Is form permanent or transitory? And are sensation, perception, predispositions, and consciousness permanent or transitory?"

"They are transitory," replied the five.

"And is transitory evil or good?"

"Evil," they replied.

"Then can it be said of what is transitory, evil, and subject to change, 'This is "Mine," "I," "Myself" '?"

"No, this cannot be said," replied the five.

"Therefore, brethren, it must be admitted of every kind of physical form, past, present, or future, subjective or objective, distant or near, high or low, that 'This is not Mine, this is not I, this is not Myself.' And similarly it must be said of all sensations, perceptions, predispositions, and consciousness, 'These are not Mine, these are not I, these are not Myself.'

"And being aware of this, brethren, the true disciple will develop a disgust for physical form, for sensation, perception, predispositions, and consciousness. And so he will be stripped of desire. He becomes freed thereby and becomes aware of this freedom. And he knows that becoming has ended, that he has lived in purity, that he has done his duty and has forever ended mortality." *Samyutta-Nikaya*

THE FIRE SERMON

All things, brethren, are burning. And what are all these things that are burning? The eye is on fire, forms are on fire, eye consciousness is on fire, the eye's impressions are on fire. And also on fire are all sensations originating from seeing—pleasant, unpleasant, or neutral.

And with what are all these burning? With fires of lust, hatred, and illusion; with birth, old age, death, mourning, misery, grief, and despair.

It is the same with the ear, the nose, tongue, and sense of touch. The mind also is on fire, thoughts are on fire. The conscious brain and impressions received by the brain, together with the sensations stirred by these, are also on fire.

With what are they burning? I say they are burning with the fires of lust, of hatred, and illusion. They are burning with the fires of birth, old age, sorrow, mourning, misery, grief, and despair.

Realizing this, brethren, the true disciple gets a disgust for the eye, for forms, for eye consciousness, for the eye's impressions, and the sensations thus arising. He also conceives disgust for the ear, nose, tongue, sense of touch, mind, thoughts, mind consciousness, impressions, and sensations.

Thus stripped of desire he is aware that he is freed. He knows there will be no more becoming, that he has lived in purity, that he has done his duty, and forever ended mortality. *Samyutta-Nikaya*

THE CAVERN CALLED THE BODY

He who is enslaved to that cavern we call the body is unhappy. The cavern is darkened by delusion and unsatisfied craving; and the pleasures of this world are hard to give up.

Those who try to re-live past pleasures, or ambitiously to plan future pleasures, are creatures of craving and slaves of joy. They cannot be helped, because one cannot be freed by another. A man can be saved only by himself.

Those blindly pursuing pleasure become mean and selfish. They run into disaster and then cry: "What will happen to us? What is to be our fate in rebirth?"

The wise say that life is short; so realize this now: You know that baseness is base—so renounce baseness.

See how those poor wretches, the worldly men, tremble. They cling to life, then shrink from death.

See how the worldly men struggle after their paltry ambitions. They are like fish in a stream that is fast running dry. Realizing this, we should live with unselfishness in this life and stop worrying about the next life.

The wise man stays indifferent to what he sees and hears. For he overcomes craving for the present and the future; he lives without desire; he is incapable of any evil action.

The tranquil man of wisdom fares well over life's flood of sorrows, for he is unhandicapped by desire and craving. He has extracted the arrow of the passions; and he remains indifferent to everything, both of this world and the next.

Guhatthaka Sutta

LOVE ALL-EMBRACING

The true disciple who is striving towards the Highest, lets his mind pervade all quarters of the world with thoughts of love; first one quarter, and so the second, and so the third, and so the fourth quarter. And thus the whole wide world, above, below, around, and everywhere does he pervade with a heart of love, far-reaching, grown great and beyond measure.

Just as a great trumpeter makes himself heard without difficulty in all four directions, he does not pass by or leave aside anything possessing form or life. He looks at them all with a mind set free, a mind filled with deep-felt love.

Truly, this is the way to a state of union with the Highest. He lets his mind pervade one quarter of the world with thoughts of pity, sympathy, and equanimity, and then on to the second, the third, and the fourth. And thus throughout the world, above, below, around, and everywhere he continues to pervade with a pitiful heart, with sympathy, and equanimity, far-reaching, beyond measure, and all embracing.

Just as that great trumpeter makes himself heard without difficulty in all four directions, he does not pass by or leave aside anything possessing form or life. He looks at them all with deep-felt pity, sympathy, and equanimity.

Truly, this is the way to a state of oneness with the Highest. *Tevijja Sutta*

HONEST DOUBT

Don't believe anything on mere hearsay.

Don't believe traditions because they happen to be old and have been passed down through many generations.

Don't believe anything because people talk a lot about it.

Don't believe solely because the written testimony of some ancient wise man is shown to you.

Never believe anything that begs to be taken for granted, or because ancient precedent tempts you to regard it as true.

And don't believe anything on the mere authority of your teachers or priests.

What you *should* accept as true and as the guide to your life is whatever agrees with your own reason and your own experience after thorough investigation, and whatever is helpful both to your own well-being and that of other living beings. *Anguttara-Nikaya*

TRUTH AS A LAMP

The Buddha was approaching death when he said to his disciple Ananda:

"I have reached the sum of my days. I am turning eighty years of age.

"Just as a worn-out cart cannot be made to move without much difficulty, so the body of the Tathagata can only be kept going with a lot of additional care.

"It is only when the Tathagata, ceasing to pay attention to any outward thing, becomes plunged into devout meditation which is concerned with no bodily object, that the body of the Tathagata is at ease.

"Therefore, Ananda, you must be lamps unto yourselves. Rely upon yourselves. Do not rely upon external help.

"Hold fast to the truth as a lamp. Seek salvation alone in the truth. Look not for help to any one besides yourselves." *Mahaparinibbana Sutta*

ATTAINMENT OF GOOD

All that we are is the result of what we have thought. It is founded on our thoughts; it is made up of our thoughts.

Everything that we are is the result of what we have thought. Everything that we are is based on our thoughts, formed from our thoughts. When a man speaks or acts with pure thought, then happiness follows him like his ever-present shadow.

"He reviled me, struck me, defeated me, and then robbed me." Those who have such thoughts paralyze their minds with desire for revenge. In them hatred never ceases.

"He reviled me, struck me, defeated me, and then robbed me." In those who never have such thoughts, hatred ceases.

Hatred does not cease by hatred. Hatred ceases by love. This is the eternal law.

Even though others do not understand the folly of conflict, let us avoid it. But quarrels will cease among those who do understand.

He who pursues pleasure, whose senses are uncontrolled, who is immoderate in eating, idle, and weak, will be overthrown by Mara (the Evil One) as the storm tears down a weak tree.

He who does not pursue pleasure, whose senses are controlled, who eats moderately, who is devoted and diligent, cannot be overthrown by the Evil One, as a storm cannot tear down a mountain peak.

He who has donned the Yellow Robe without taking care to purify his mind, to gain sense-control and wisdom, is unworthy of that Robe.

He who has donned the Yellow Robe while taking care to purify his mind, to gain sense-control and wisdom, is worthy of that Robe.

Those living in the pleasure gardens of imagination see truth in the false and untruth in the real. They never reach truth.

Those who live in the world of right thinking see truth in the real and falsity in the unreal. They reach truth.

As rain leaks into a badly roofed house, so desire leaks into an ill-trained mind.

As rain fails to leak into a well-roofed house, so desire fails to leak into a well-trained mind.

The evil-doer grieves both in this existence and in the next. He grieves in the realization of his bad deeds.

The virtuous man rejoices both in this existence and in the next. His rejoicing increases in the realization of his good deeds.

The evil-doer mourns in both existences. "I have done wrong," he tells himself. He grieves more when he has moved into an evil existence.

The virtuous man is happy in both existences. "I have done well," he tells himself. His joy becomes greater when he has moved into a blissful existence.

The man who talks piously but does not live up to his words is like a cowherd tending the cattle of others. He has no share in the blessings of the noble life.

The man sharing such blessings is he who abandons lust, hatred, and folly, who, possessing true knowledge and a serene mind, talks little but lives up to the Teaching.

Dhammapada

THE MIND

Just as a fletcher planes an arrow, so does the wise man plane the unsteady mind which is difficult to strengthen and to discipline.

As a fish flaps around when pulled from its watery home and thrown on the bank, so our mind struggles and shivers to escape the dominion of the Evil One.

It is good to restrain the mind when it jumps from object to object, out of control. A well-trained mind brings happiness.

A wise man should watch his thinking. The mind moves with such subtlety, wandering here and there wherever it likes. To watch the mind brings happiness.

He who controls the mind will escape the bondage of the Evil One. The mind is bodiless, strays about alone, and dwells in the heart.

Wisdom will not enter the mind of one who lacks confidence and who is ignorant of the true Teaching.

Fear will not come to the man whose mind is not burning with desires, who, rising above likes and dislikes, is awakened.

Realizing that his body is as fragile as a clay pot, and making a fortress of his mind, he should fight the Evil One with the sword of wisdom. And while guarding what he has gained, he should fight on.

Very soon the body will lie on the ground, cast aside and empty of consciousness, as useless as a log of wood.

The misery wrought by a malicious man, by an enemy to his enemy, is nothing in comparison to the misery following one with a wrongly directed mind.

Neither father nor mother, nor any other relative, can do a man greater service than his own well-directed mind.

Dhammapada

APPENDIX

THE FOUR NOBLE TRUTHS (*see page 2*)

1. The Noble Truth Concerning Suffering
2. The Noble Truth Concerning the Arising of Suffering
3. The Noble Truth Concerning the Cessation of Suffering
4. The Noble Truth Concerning the Way to the Cessation of Suffering

THE EIGHTFOLD PATH (*see pages 41–46*)

1. Right View
2. Right Resolution
3. Right Speech
4. Right Conduct
5. Right Livelihood
6. Right Effort
7. Right Mindfulness
8. Right Concentration

THE THREE SIGNS OF BEING (*see page 58*)

1. Impermanence
2. Suffering
3. Non-self

THE TEN FETTERS (*see page 62*)

1. Delusion of Self
2. Doubt
3. Belief in the Efficacy of Ceremonies and Ritual
4. Sensuality
5. Ill-will
6. Passion for Earthly Life
7. Desire for Future Life
8. Pride
9. Self-righteousness
10. Ignorance

THE LAW OF DEPENDENT ORIGINATION

(*see page 74*)

From ignorance come the dispositions which lead to rebirth.
From the dispositions comes consciousness or cognition.
From consciousness come name and form (personality).
From name and form come the five senses and the mind.
From the five senses and the mind comes contact.
From contact comes feeling.
From feeling comes craving.
From craving comes grasping, or attachment to existence.
From grasping comes becoming.
From becoming comes birth.
From birth come old age, sickness, death.

BIBLIOGRAPHY

Dwight Goddard: *A Buddhist Bible.*
Francis Story: *Sangiti; The Case for Rebirth.*
F. Harold Smith: *The Buddhist Way of Life.*
Christmas Humphreys: *Buddhism.*
Edwin Arnold: *The Light of Asia.*
Hugh Fausset: *The Flame and the Light.*
E. A. Burtt: *Teachings of the Compassionate Buddha.*
Bhadragaka: *New Translation of the Dhammapada.*
Ananda Coomaraswamy: *Buddha and the Gospel of Budhism.*
N. Gangalee: *The Buddha and His Message.*
Paul Dahlke: *Buddhist Essays.*
T. W. Rhys Davids: *Buddhism* (American Lectures); *Budhism; Early Buddhism.*
Mrs. Rhys Davids: *Buddhism; Manual of Buddhism; Poems of Cloister and Jungle.*
Edmund Holmes: *Creed of the Buddha.*
F. L. Woodward: *Some Sayings of the Buddha.*
Paul Carus: *Gospel of the Buddha.*

Maurice Percheron: *Buddha and Buddhism.*

Ronald Fussell: *The Buddha and His Path to Self-Enlightenment.*

E. Conze: *Buddhist Texts Throughout the Ages.*

L. Adams Beck: *Life of the Buddha.*

A. H. Bahm: *Philosophy of the Buddha.*

Edward J. Thomas: *Life of the Buddha as Legend and History.*

Hermann Oldenberg: *Buddha.*

E. H. Brewster: *The Life of Gotama the Buddha.*

Radhakumud Mookerji: *Asoka.*

Vincent Smith: *Asoka, Buddhist Emperor of India.*

R. S. Copleston: *Buddhism Primitive and Present in Magadha and Ceylon.*

E. F. C. Ludowyk: *Footprint of the Buddha.*

H. Fielding Hall: *The Soul of a People.*

E. H. Shattock: *An Experiment in Mindfulness.*

Leslie Weatherhead: *The Case for Reincarnation.*

Heinrich Zimmer: *Philosophies of India.*

Publications of the Pali Text Society, London.

Booklets of Buddhist Publication Society, Ceylon.

Booklets and Pamphlets of the Buddhist Society, London.

INDEX